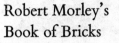

Robert Morley's Book of Bricks

Robert Morley was born in what is now Julian Bream's house at
Semley in Wiltshire in 1908. Originally intended for the
diplomatic service, or so he has always told himself, he in fact
ended up on the stage where he first appeared as a pirate in
Treasure Island in 1929. Since that time he has appeared in more
than fifty plays, many of them his own, and nearly a hundred
films, many of which he cannot remember. The first British actor
to play Oscar Wilde on the stage and screen, he is probably best
remembered for performances in *The Man Who Came to Dinner,
Edward My Son, Hippo Dancing* and more recently Alan
Ayckbourn's *How The Other Half Loves* and Ben Travers' *Banana
Ridge.* His most recent stage play is *Picture of Innocence* and on film
he was recently to be found in *Someone Is Killing The Great
Chefs of Europe.*

A regular contributor to *Punch, Playboy* and the *Times Literary
Supplement,* Robert Morley lives in Berkshire with his wife and
many other relatives.

edited and compiled by Robert Morley

Robert Morley's
Book of Bricks

illustrations by Geoffrey Dickinson and John Jensen

Pan Books London and Sydney

This book is dedicated to the autistic children
all over the world who drop bricks and sometimes hurl them,
on whose behalf it has been compiled.

First published in Great Britain 1978 by Weidenfeld & Nicolson Ltd
This edition published 1979 by Pan Books Ltd,
Cavaye Place, London SW10 9PG
© Weidenfeld & Nicolson Ltd 1978
All royalties to the National Society for Autistic Children
ISBN 0 330 25881 8
Printed and bound in Great Britain by
Hazell Watson & Viney Ltd, Aylesbury, Bucks

Contents

Preface

ROBERT MORLEY

Except in the curious case described by William Franklyn, people don't drop bricks on purpose, the implied criticism or insult is never intentional. Indeed, nearly all bricks fall on the toes of friends and acquaintances to whom we are making a conscious effort to extend the hand of friendship. Anxiety to please, to put another at ease, is the banana skin on which we slide and fall headlong. In my own case the story of my encounter with the wife of Alan Delon exactly illustrates the point. 'Heavens,' I told myself, 'I must keep off the subject of murder at all costs,' and found, to my horror, I was enquiring politely the exact manner in which she was accustomed to fire a revolver. Sometimes, as in this case, one recovers all too swiftly from the embarrassment and before the day is out one is almost boasting of one's own clumsiness.

I have recounted the Delon story often, each time embellishing the tale as is my wont. On the other hand, I have never quite been able to forgive myself for my encounter with the lady behind the counter in the draper's shop, though this incident must have occurred close on fifty years ago. In the first case I was trying to please, in the second trying to show off, a more culpable fault. Lest this introduction proves over-virtuous, I should point out how much I usually enjoy brick-dropping and how pleased I am that my own talent in this direction seldom falters.

Brick-droppers in this book fall, I think, into three categories. In the first category is the persistent offender, who more often than not is a man like myself, unduly absorbed in his own affairs so that casual remarks become altogether too casual. Besides myself, Sir John Gielgud, whose feats are recorded throughout these pages, is someone who is usually thinking of something else when he is actually speaking.

'Do you understand what you say?' asks a character in one of Oscar Wilde's plays, of his child. 'Yes, father,' comes the reply, 'but only if I listen very carefully.' The sentence attributed to Gielgud on visiting the newly acquired flat of a lifelong friend: 'Dear Boy, how sensible of you to move to town, I too should give up my absurd house and move into an apartment,' is fine if left at that, but to continue: 'Mind you I couldn't bear a pokey little place like this,' argues the speaker is now once again too closely concerned with his own affairs.

In the second category are the compulsive compliment-payers who snatch at a thought and turn it into praise without realizing the pitfalls of such over-enthusiasm. Thus Ambrosine Phillpotts, wishing to express her admiration of a friend for inviting her and her family to lunch: 'I have told the children that whatever the food is like they are not to complain,' reveals only too clearly her misgivings over the culinary abilities of a good neighbour.

Compliments must, if they are to be successful, be thought out in advance. My own approach to a neighbour at a luncheon party which started impeccably, 'I do envy you living in Australia, so few of we British have the sense to cut and run,' could never have stood up in this context. Realizing that my opening phrase might suggest some sort of criminal activity, I felt obliged to expand the sentence and enquire as to his exact occupation, thus pouring oil on what I felt might become troubled waters and letting him understand fully that I was aware he was not an absconding banker. It was pure bad luck that the man I happened to interrogate in this way was a Governor General, who reminded me I had already been introduced twice over cocktails.

Because I am an actor, strangers rightly suppose I wish to talk about myself and often helpfully provide the cues to enable me to do just that. On the other hand, as there is a sort of hopeless inevitability about my embarking on my stories and as I don't immediately wish to be asked whether I prefer acting in films or in the theatre (dreading my answer as much as they will at length regret having asked it), I try to fend off such early questions by asking people what they do. It is my misfortune that I almost invariably pick on world-famous painters, musicians or politicians, of whose identity and achievements I am usually profoundly ignorant.

It is no good pretending, for instance, that classical guitarist Julian Bream or ex-Premier of Australia Mr McMahon really enjoy this kind of imposed anonymity any more than I should – it is all right for a few seconds but it should not be allowed to last. My own most sustained attack in this direction occurred in Australia: while I was waiting in the collecting ring outside a television studio before appearing on a chat show, I espied the fellow incautiously seated beside a banjo. Now, on these occasions there is always among the performers one 'Musso', as they say out there, who is actually to be paid for his appearance – the rest of us receiving our reward in the less tangible form of exposure. Usually I am there not entirely for personal aggrandizement but to sell such merchandise as I am currently hawking – a new book or, as in this case, a play. With only the banjo separating us, I proceeded to compliment Mr McMahon on his astuteness in demanding and receiving dollars for his participation on this occasion. For some reason, either because I am deaf or because Mr McMahon muttered, I failed to hear his disclaimer that he was not a music-maker but a politician who had only recently lost an election and with it the Premiership. I understood only that he was a retired politico who had recently turned professional banjo-playing into a lucrative calling. 'How wise of you to get out of politics,' I assured him, 'I hear most of the politicos here are pretty crook.'

Having started on the wrong track, I persisted into the wind of his remonstrance, even when he assured me he had been Prime Minister. 'How splendid!' I told him, 'I am sure you had got all you could in that field. How much more rewarding to start afresh. Do you find people come to hear you play because you were once Prime Minister? We have the same situation roughly with Edward Heath in my country, only, of course, I suppose he is still in the game more or less.'

The moment came when my victim broke under the strain: 'Do

I have to listen to this any longer?' he asked of no one in particular and bolted into the recording studio, leaving his instrument behind. 'He's forgotten his banjo,' I told the others who remained. 'Should I take it to him?' 'It is a guitar, not a banjo, and it happens to be mine,' one of the real 'Mussos' told me, and I realized I had dropped my brick for the day. As for poor Mr McMahon, he was so unnerved by the incident that he spent the first few moments of what he had intended to be, I imagine, a political broadcast bewailing the fact that one of his children had a bad case of trench mouth. 'Of course you did it on purpose,' friends still tell me when I recount this story of which, naturally, I never tire.

The third category of brick-droppers, those who are neither so preoccupied with their own thoughts nor yet so anxious to create *bonhomie*, are the people who are not even trying to break the ice through which they subsequently fall. In this category the most amusing bricks were sent to me by members of the general public in response to a competition that I announced on television. The competition entries were, on the whole, concerned with two kinds of dropped bricks: chance malapropisms and *double entendres*. If my competition correspondents are to be believed, 'tentacles' are constantly being confused with 'testicles', 'organisms' with 'orgasms', and any sentence in which the words 'balls' or 'privates' occur almost invariably leads to embarrassment. The story of the dog at the front door (p. 104), to the sender of which I awarded a small prize, was, I discovered later, unlikely to have faced such a dilemma personally as the tale subsequently turned up again and again. In the same way, stories of cricket boxes and French letters submitted by one-time shop assistants would, if I had included them all, have filled this book many times over, so I have selected only a token example of each and hope that the many other kind correspondents will not feel I have stolen their thunder.

It is surprising, too, how often the words 'organ' and 'erection' are juxtaposed by unwitting speakers. Mr Hodder, a fellow Old Wellingtonian, provided an amusing instance of this and because his letter also contained a typical example of the over-exuberant trap

I have printed it in full (page 49), which is, alas, more than space permitted me to do with most of the competition entries gratefully received.

The introduction of a visiting speaker by the chairman is a positive minefield for the unwary. A correspondent who prefers anonymity rather than run the risk of embarrassing a friend recalls the latter introducing a distinguished cleric about to address the conference as 'the venereal Archdeacon'.

My friend, Michael Noakes, gives a splendid example of a Spoonerism while painting Her Majesty; and possibly because my late father-in-law invented the cocktail, I am attracted by the unwary waitress asking the wedding guest whether he would partake of a 'Fuck's Bizz'. I like too the contribution sent in by Mrs Hakeman whose unenviable task it was once to sit at the telephone hour after hour attempting to drum up business for a firm bearing the name 'County Craftwork', until, of course, the inevitable Spoonerism became a matter of dread and she was obliged to resign the task before she announced too frequently to prospective customers that she represented 'Crafty Cuntwork'.

I have avoided the accounts of bricks dropped by children but cannot forbear to include in this introduction the story of the youth for whose piles the doctor prescribed suppositories, instructing him where to put them as soon as he got home; when his mother arrived home with a friend for tea, she found the suppositories already unpacked and neatly arranged in line from the backdoor to the kitchen. This gives me a chance to tell, tastefully I trust, of a misadventure of Mrs Robards of Bedford, who, as a child, had her temperature taken and, when her mother stopped the car on the way home from the surgery to have the oil checked, she asked the garage proprietor if he wasn't going to put Vaseline on the dip-stick.

The classroom, particularly the medical one, has produced a great number of bricks, and I am grateful to Mrs Woolf who found herself teaching about the skin and the fact that most of it is covered in hair, when one of her teenage pupils enquired why he was going bald at an early age: 'It must be in your genes,' she told him before noticing 'his' dress. Later, she informed a class of Chinese students that the first sign of liver failure was for the skin to turn yellow, which raises the question, how does a Chinese doctor diagnose jaundice? I like too the reply of a Brownie pack leader who does not wish her name included in the tale but who had to report to the police a gentleman exposing himself to her pack; pressed for a description of the man, she said that she hadn't been looking at his face.

On the other hand, Mr Andreasson, writing to me from Manchester, described a party he attended at which he remarked (I quote verbatim): '"I wonder who the first person will be to drop their pants, which is quite common at this type of party." Unfortunately [he continues] and unknown to myself, one of my fellow guests had just appeared in court for exposing himself and naturally the room went rather quiet until the strains of Chuck Berry's latest record "I want you to play with my ding-a-ling" cheered us all up once more.'

A Mrs Barker sent me a tale which is, I fear, apocryphal, of a school outing to Doncaster when a teacher instructed her charges not to bother with the Gents' toilet on this occasion, but to go behind the fence. The smallest child at the back seemed in no hurry, so she helpfully undid his flies, and then looking up said with some astonishment, 'I don't know you, you're not in my class.' 'No, Ma'am,' he replied, 'I'm Scobie Breasley.'

Any number of stories concern the brick-dropper in the matter of colour. My own favourite was told of the late Ivor Novello: grasping Miss Elizabeth Welch's hand during an ecstatic curtain speech, he said, 'I am so glad you enjoyed it, we have all worked like blacks.'

I am deeply grateful to Desmond Morris, whose sparkling dissertation I am proud to include in this collection. His explanation of the Freudian slip is particularly interesting and may account for why so many letters recall such incidents: visiting Nigerians at cocktail parties, so often urged to have a coconut rather than a Coca-Cola, and bald gentlemen in banks sporting, in what in my trade are called mats, being asked whether they want to cash their wigs.

I wish I could believe that Mrs Gregory really did happen to have her specimen of urine handy on the hall table when a gentleman from the waterworks rang the bell, but I am convinced we are on firmer ground in revealing that Pete Murray once asked the badly scarred Nicki Lauda, recently escaped from a blazing racing car, whether he had any other burning ambitions, or commenting on a young actress's account of how she had once stayed unwittingly in a brothel that it must have been 'a right cock-up'.

Christopher Headington, in charge of BBC Music presentation, avoided similar *contretemps*, alas, by not reading out two programme notes supplied by his assistants: 'Amahl grabs his crutch and hurls himself on the Page' and 'This aria is traditionally sung by the heroine Agathe, while waiting for her lover to come.' I am indebted to Mr Burnett, too, whose sharp ears picked up Donald Houston's opening gambit on a chat show: when asked whether he thought the survivors of a recent appalling air crash were justified in resorting to cannibalism in order to survive, 'I think,' he told us simply, 'they started off on the wrong foot.'

What was to prove a rather expensive brick was dropped by David O. Selznick when watching the great couturier Monsieur Givenchy deck out his wife for a picture called *Beat the Devil*. We were about to start shooting in Ravello. Although it was not one of his own productions, the great interferer, as he was known in the industry, had decided Jennifer's wardrobe must outdo that of Gina Lollobrigida, her fellow star, and so he had summoned the maître from Paris. Monsieur Givenchy arrived breathless and exhausted, but bearing the hastily stitched toiles. 'How clever of you, Monsieur,' Selznick told the astonished couturier, 'to dress my wife entirely in white.' Monsieur Givenchy wisely took his money and ran, leaving the Wardrobe Department to cope as best they could.

I should like to thank, once more, all the people who have contributed to this book, and Lord Weidenfeld who has ensured that so large a portion of the profits will be given to the National Society for Autistic Children, and particularly my researcher, Miss Jane Myerson, whose tireless enthusiasm, elegant typing and cheerful encouragement have made it all come true.

Introduction

DESMOND MORRIS

ON DROPPING A BRICK

The quiet man in the corner may be thinking great thoughts, his golden silence too rich to share with the bores that surround him, or he may simply be shy. One of the main roots of shyness is the fear of making a social blunder, and it is a fear that can reach such proportions that it may lead to a major withdrawal from the social scene. For most of us, happily, this extreme condition is never experienced – except, perhaps, as brief moments of panic when we wish the floor would swallow us up. Immediately after dropping a brick at a social gathering there is nothing we would like better than an instantaneous, magical withdrawal from the whole of society, until the pain has dulled. But instead we try to pass it off and become heavily preoccupied with other matters. Inwardly we may go on feeling our pangs of embarrassment, but outwardly, somehow, we keep going. Later, sometimes many years later, merely to recall that terrible moment of the great *faux pas* is enough to make us groan inwardly at the tactless blunder we committed.

If our social gaffes are so painful, why do we let them happen? What is it that momentarily breaks through our usual control of good manners and everyday etiquette? The answer is complicated because there are several different kinds of bricks to be dropped. I think there are seven, but there may well be more. The seven I know are as follows:

1. *The Freudian Brick* Better known as the Freudian slip, this one is the psychoanalyst's delight. Freud first wrote about it at the turn of the century and, although it has become a popular concept, like many of his ideas, it is only half-understood. A simple example

would be: a young man takes a girl into a restaurant and asks the head waiter, 'Do you have a room?' What he means to say, of course, is, 'Do you have a table?', but he has something other than food on his mind and the wrong word comes to the surface. He is already imagining the girl in bed with him, after the meal, and the idea of a bedroom is so preoccupying him that the word 'room' breaks loose and floats out into the embarrassed air.

That is the simple explanation of a Freudian slip, but it misses out something. The point is that he was not thinking about the bedroom scene at the moment of uttering the word 'room'. His anticipation of sexual-delights-to-come was swirling around in his mind long before the fateful brick was dropped. So why did the secret preoccupation choose that particular moment to break surface? Why was it the word 'table' that was to be the victim of the blunder? He and the girl had been chatting together for some time. Hundreds of words had already been spoken, any one of which might have been the 'replaced word'. The psychoanalytical explanation is that there was also something special about the word 'table'. It was not only the word 'room' that wanted to surface, it was also the word 'table' that wanted to sink. So, to say that the young man was thinking about sex is only half the story. He was also in some way against the idea of sitting down at a table with the girl. There are many possible reasons for this. Perhaps he could ill afford the meal, but he felt he had to go through the ritual of entertaining the girl before making further advances. This might give him mild, repressed resentment about the whole business of going into a restaurant and asking for a table. Or there might be some other hidden fear he was suppressing – not knowing the correct way to order the food in French from the menu, or some other seemingly trivial etiquette anxiety.

All this may seem unnecessarily complicated, but it does help to give us better insight as to why one particular word becomes the victim of a verbal slip. The next time you hear one, it is worth looking beyond the obvious – the 'wrong' word used – and to ask what was special about the 'right' word that was supplanted. You may find it tells you twice as much about the Freudian brick-dropper.

2. *The Absent-minded Brick* In one of Jacques Tati's films, a passenger in a car lights his cigarette with the car-lighter, casually shakes it as if extinguishing the flame of a match and then equally casually throws it out of the window. As with the Freudian slip, preoccupation is the villain of this piece. If our mind is on other things, our behaviour often becomes a shade too automatic. We go into a set pattern – lighting a cigarette – and ignore the special details of this particular instance of lighting it. It may, of course, be that we are unconsciously envious of the driver's expensive motor-car with its fancy lighter, but that would be over-Freuding the blunder. It is easy to read too much into such acts of simple carelessness. For instance, I am left-handed and there is always the faint danger that, at a cramped dinner table, I may reach out with my left hand and take the glass of wine belonging to the guest on my left. Having done this throughout a long, formal dinner to the mounting distress of the person sitting next to me (who was too polite to comment), I am careful now not to repeat the blunder, but should I do so again it would simply mean that I was so engrossed in conversation with the person on my right, that I was unaware of what I was doing, and my hand was merely performing the simplest, most direct movement towards the nearest glass. There would be no sinister, suppressed hostility towards my victim, and a Freudian interpretation would be inappropriate. The fact is that deep concentration puts blinkers on us and we progressively shut out competing stimuli from the world around us. In this way, total engrossment can lead to serious *faux pas*.

3. *The Helpful Brick* The king enters the room and moves among the guests chatting informally. He comes to a man whose face seems familiar. In reality, it is familiar because it has been exposed a great deal on television, but the king says: 'We've met before, haven't we?' The guest is flustered because he knows that this is not true, but, not wishing to contradict the monarch, he goes into a 'white lie' routine he has used many times before: 'Let me see, perhaps it was at …' While searching verbally for a place where they might have

met, he senses the king's irritation and instantly realizes that, in being over-helpful, he has dropped a royal brick. White lies require more skilful handling than simple truths. The lie on this occasion failed to fit and became a gaffe – the precise opposite of what was intended. If the king had been a forgotten acquaintance, then it would have worked well enough, but when misapplied to the royal person it became an insult because one is not supposed to have only vague recollections of the moment when one is presented to royalty.

In this way small white lies meant to protect our companions can often lead to wildly ramifying complications – the stuff of which French farces are made.

4. *The Over-exposed Brick*   Every act we perform has a rating on a social exposure scale. At one end of the scale are the totally private acts that we only perform behind closed doors, and at the other end are the totally public acts that we perform daily on the street. In between there is a borderline area which becomes a matter of delicate etiquette. If we make an act slightly more public on this scale, while others keep it more private, then we are over-exposing and in this way we may sometimes drop a special kind of brick. The foreign guest, for example, who comes from a culture where belching is an accepted public act at the end of a meal – and may even be considered a necessary compliment to the chef – will find himself dropping a heavy brick at a Western dinner table if he gives vent to a large belch while munching the After Eight mints. To avoid this kind of gaffe, he must adjust the scale of his exposure ratings to fit the culture in which he finds himself. Clothing gaffes are common in this category – wearing something too posh, or too scruffy, for a given context. Today the trend is all towards more exposure – not of flesh necessarily, but of the more private modes of conduct. The casual clothes that once we would have worn only to slop about in in private are now accepted costume for public festivities. The trouble is that the trend is uneven and we are sometimes caught out by a surviving stronghold of formality that unexpectedly resists the general trend. In the old days the rigid rules of costume and conduct may have been tediously restrictive, but they did at least reduce the risk of this

particular kind of brick-dropping.

5. *The Accidental Brick*   At a party we accidentally tip something on the floor. Bending down to pick it up, we do not notice that our hostess has sat down in the vacant space beside us. As we are about to regain our seat, we reach out, without looking, to grasp something for support, only to find to our horror that it is our hostess's upper thigh we are holding. Such moments, although clearly accidental to both parties and to anyone watching, are nonetheless sources of acute embarrassment. The more intimate the contact made, the worse the pang that is felt whenever the moment is recalled later. One man I know still breaks out in a sweat whenever he remembers the children's party at which he tugged so hard at his aunt's skirts (he was about five at the time) that they fell down about her ankles, leaving her de-skirted in full public view. Because at the time she was the queen of the country in which this happened, the assembled adults were so horrified that the little boy's innocent accident was transformed by their shock into something terrible, and he still suffers today, many years later, whenever some chance remark makes the scene flash before him once more.

6. *The Ignorant Brick*   The man at a party who asks Yehudi Menuhin whether he is interested in music, belongs to a special category of brick-dropper: the simple, straightforward ignoramus. We all have to wear this label at least a few times in our lives. My wife once asked John Dankworth whether he liked modern jazz, and I vividly recall the moment when I asked a man at a marine conference whether he was interested in diving. 'Yes,' he said, looking faintly puzzled. 'Have you been very deep?' I asked, ignoring the danger signs flitting across his face. '35,820 feet,' replied Jacques Piccard, as he strolled away to find a less fatuous companion. We have all done it once or twice, and it is hard to forget. The blame nearly always lies with the introducer. For some reason people mumble names as if they were dirty words when introducing people at social gatherings, and this alone accounts for a huge pile of dropped bricks that could so easily have been avoided.

There is a special kind of Ignorant Brick that I have been studying lately: the gestural brick. Errors with words are well-known, but mistakes made with gestures are less understood. We all think that other people use gestures in the same way as ourselves, but this is often untrue and can get us into all kinds of unfortunate situations in foreign parts. Take the dear old British thumbs-up sign, for instance. What could be more harmless? It means all's well, OK, everything's fine. Surely this would be understood everywhere in the world? Well, no, not quite everywhere. Unfortunately, in some countries, like Sardinia and parts of the Middle East, it is an obscene insult and means roughly 'sit on this!'. I have watched British hitch-hikers in southern Sardinia standing by the side of the road, jerking their thumbs at passing cars and cursing when they failed to stop. What the hitchhikers were in fact saying to the passing motorists was not 'give us a lift', but 'up yours', and the faces of the angry drivers should have given them a clue that something was wrong. No, in many countries, the way to ask for a lift is with a limply waved, flattened hand.

Then there is the famous American OK sign, the ring gesture made by thumb and forefinger. This, too, is an obscenity in some places, and I don't advise its use if you happen to be on holiday in Turkey. In France, to confuse matters further, it can also mean 'zero' or worthless – just the opposite of the message we are used to. So it is best to employ some other sign of approval when tasting the local wine.

The reverse happens with our own homegrown insult gesture, the 'Harvey Smith'. This two-finger sign can be used endlessly at Italian drivers who cut in front of your holiday vehicle, but all you will get in reply is a happy wave – for to them it means only 'peace' and 'victory', and it is not distinguished from the Churchillian war-time sign.

In Greece there is another little problem to do with a local gesture called the *moutza*. In this a flat hand is raised, palm towards the victim and pushed towards him as if about to thrust an invisible custard pie in his face. To us it simply looks like a 'go back, go back' signal, but to any Greek it is a hideous insult. It dates from Byzantine times, when the prisoners were paraded in chains through the streets and the people abused them by picking up handfuls of filth from the gutter and thrusting it into the faces of the helpless captives. The practice ceased centuries ago, but the savage message of the *moutza* gesture survives in Greece to this day.

Ignorance of these gestural differences can easily lead to the same kind of embarrassment as the more familiar verbal blunders, and one can't help wondering how many times local inhabitants have been too polite to tell their visitors what terrible gaffes they have been committing during the course of their happy-go-lucky package tours.

7. *The Deliberate Brick* Deliberate bricks, I suspect, are more common in the movies than in real life. The man who spills coffee on the girl's dress so that she will have to take it off for cleaning is bold enough to be a social rarity. Occasionally, there emerges from the woodwork a cruelly cynical character who stalks the social scene, dropping calculated bricks to embarrass and dismay, but he soon becomes isolated, unless, of course, he is a man of great power or influence. For most of us, the brick remains, happily, a blunder we desperately try to avoid. Sometimes we try so hard that the very process of trying preoccupies us to the point where we trip up over our own effort. But, thank goodness, for the most part, we sail merrily through the minefield of social occasions with hardly a scratch on our paintwork. This, of course, is what makes the occasional lapses so glaringly conspicuous, so conversation-stopping, so breath-grabbing, and so long recalled and winced over.

The people who have willingly recounted their worst gaffes in this book have been generous indeed to share their private agonies and convert their worst moments into shared smiles and outright belly-laughs. Perhaps in the act of sharing they will at last be able to lay the ghosts of blunders past. . . .

Michael Holroyd

BIOGRAPHER

I have dined only once with a member of the Royal Family. She was a marvellous mimic. First we had a rich North Country accent, then a perfect take-off of Edna O'Brien's plaintive Irish. Being slightly nervous, I allowed my appreciation to get rather out-of-hand. Again she spoke and this time I outdid myself, braying with laughter, applauding, congratulating, 'Do it again, Ma'am,' I urged. 'That one's *priceless*.' Suddenly I noticed that there was silence round the table and everyone was staring at me. She had been talking in her own voice.

with acknowledgements to H.M. BATEMAN.

Denis Norden

SCRIPTWRITER AND BROADCASTER

'Doing it that way,' I said to Peter Scott, the naturalist, in the course of idle conversation, 'you can kill two birds with one stone.'

Robert's request to sweep up some of my brick-dropping brought it home to me that, after what seems a lifetime in the service of *gaucherie*, I've probably done for the art of social interaction what the film *Jaws* did for swimming.

'Hey, what happened to that skinny blonde your husband used to be married to?' I asked this nice lady at a party. After a pause, she said, 'I dyed my hair.'

It's at parties that the dull thud is most frequently heard. I was only formally introduced to Christiaan Barnard after I'd advised him what to do for his cold. At another gathering I casually asked Andy Stewart if he was doing anything on New Year's Eve. In the course of similar cocktail chat, 'Neither a borrower nor a lender be,' I quoted to a foreign gentleman who turned out to be a distinguished banker. And, on the same collision course, I used the phrase 'stick to your guns', while trying to express to Canon Collins my wholehearted support for his ideals.

Shall I go on about the lady down the road who asked me to bring back something decorative from Geneva that she could give her son for his new offices? It was only after I'd handed her the cuckoo-clock I remembered he was a psychiatrist.

They say – and I suppose it is one of the purposes of this book – that we all profit from our mistakes. If there were any kind of truth in that, I would be one of the richest men in town.

William Hayter

DIPLOMAT AND AUTHOR

Half-way through his time as Ambassador in Cairo, Sir Miles Lampson became Lord Killearn. Not long afterwards, a visitor lunching with the Ambassador and his wife said, 'It's so nice you're here now and not those Lampsons whom everybody disliked so much.'

William Douglas Home

PLAYWRIGHT

My father – approached at some public function by a lady pushing a man in a wheelchair. 'Lord Home,' she cried keenly, 'could you possibly open our fête?' (on some date months ahead). My father stood tapping his head gently with a forefinger, trying to recall whether the suggested date was free. 'No, no,' said the lady sharply, 'he's quite all right there – it's only his legs.'

Myself – under instructions from my wife to join great friends for dinner. Having been to Oxford for a matinée, I duly arrived, dined, chatted and then rose to go around eleven.

'Thank you, Rachel, for a lovely dinner,' said my host to my wife.

'What do you mean?' I enquired. 'I brought it over from home,' Rachel explained, 'as their cook was off.'

'In that case,' I said, 'I am at liberty to say that the fish was the most disgusting thing I've ever eaten.'

'That was the only dish I provided,' said my host.

 I am reminded of another of my bricks. When lunching with William recently, he told me that he had engaged Alfred Marks for a leading part in his latest play. I replied, 'I've always admired Mr Marks tremendously – unfortunately the poor fellow always seems to choose the wrong play.'

Yehudi Menuhin

MUSICIAN

Never notorious for remembering names, nor for precision in human relationships at the social level, I am the terror of my wife, Diana, who hovers anxiously within earshot whenever I am accosted by anyone, ready to leap forward either to prompt me with a quickly hissed name and a gabbled *curriculum vitae* or to drown as loudly as she can the misnomer I have produced with shining pride.

So it is quite logical that my crowning effort in this field of social misdemeanour and muddle should have been achieved some years ago when Diana was in Florence (our headquarters at that time with Bernard Berenson) remaining with the two boys, while I was for a week in London for a batch of concerts.

Having as yet no house there – I was at Claridges and anxious to practise the coming recital with Louis Kentner – I cast around in my mind for a nearby house containing a piano. My memory for addresses being only slightly superior to my memory for names, I told Miss Smith, my long-time and long-suffering secretary, to look up a local lady of whose name unfortunately I could only recall the first half (privately I felt this to be something of a triumph): 'That nice musical lady called Aber-something,' I said to the bewildered Miss Smith, 'who lives in the vicinity.'

Used to such poor clues and nothing daunted, she reached for the A–D telephone book, during which time my groping brain suddenly grabbed at 'Abercrombie'. 'No,' she said, 'that is somewhere you occasionally get your socks in New York: Abercrombie and Fitch.' Deflated, I waited while she rifled the pages searching for a titled 'Aber ...' dwelling in West One.

'Could it be the Duchess of Abercorn?' she offered. 'She lives in Mount Street.'

Now, Diana had tried to teach me how to disentangle the ingrown complexities of British titles – not, I might add, with noticeable success. I remembered that one does not use in speaking either 'Viscountess' or 'Countess', so triumphantly I figured out that the same odd discretion would be applicable to a duchess – this must indeed be my Lady Aber ... with a piano in Mayfair.

'Do get her on the telephone,' I said, very pleased with myself. She did so; a butler answered. 'Is that the Duchess of Abercorn's house?' Miss Smith inquired and, when answered in the affirmative, added, 'I'm speaking on behalf of Mr Yehudi Menuhin, who would like to speak to Her Grace.'

A short silence ensued: 'I'm afraid not,' came the reply, 'Her Grace died last month.'

She was, I am glad to say, a very old lady, but gladder still was I that I had been saved from an embarrassing conversation with a total stranger. For, after that signal failure, I lost the courage to attack any more listed 'Aber...s' and, trusting to my memory for places, I walked up Brook Street, across Grosvenor Square, turned smartly into North Audley Street, recognized one of the last remaining lovely Georgian houses and rang the bell hopefully, but a little apprehensively.

The door was opened by the Italian butler: 'Signor Menuhin,' he cried with lovely Italian fervour. '*Che sor-*

presa! Devo subito dire a La Contessa.'

Cheered by this first sign that I had struck the right place, but still stuck with my single syllable, my heart sank when I saw the owner of the house standing at the head of the staircase. Desperate, I hissed at the butler, '*Come se chiama la Contessa?*' '*Ma*, Signor Menuhin, Lady Aber*conway*!' he hissed back.

'Yehudi, my dear,' she called out as she descended the stairs, arms outstretched... And I suppose it was her typical warmth and spontaneity that prompted the sluggish pride that is my memory and enabled me to rush into those welcoming arms and say, 'Christabel, may I use your piano?'

John Bratby

PAINTER AND WRITER

Some months ago I was married for the second time, to darling Patricia, at the Woolwich Registry Office. My former wife, to whom I had been married for twenty-five years, is called Jean Esme Oregon Cooke.

At the stage in the marriage ceremony when the ring is required for the bride's finger, Patricia, my new wife, turned and whispered to me, 'John, will you ask George [our best man] for the ring?'

Out of years of habit, I replied to her automatically, 'Yes, of course, Jean.'

Joyce Carey

ACTRESS AND PLAYWRIGHT

I am sure I must have dropped lots of bricks since, but the one I remember with a *frisson*, on account of the discomfort it must have caused, happened when I was about six or seven years old. I was staying with my grandmother in the country and the vicar's wife came to call. My granny told me to go and talk to her for a minute and say that she was coming. The vicar's wife happened to have rather a profusion of golden down on her upper lip and, having delivered my message, I said: 'Oh, Mrs Welford, how your moustache does glisten in the sun.'

I rejoice not only in the friendship of Miss Carey but also in the memory of a drive we took together in the neighbourhood of the Brecon Hills, when a third member of the party was Ambrosine Phillpotts, whose bricks are almost as legendary as Sir John Gielgud's but who, on this occasion, was listening contentedly in the back of the car to Miss Carey's reminiscences about her parents.

'Were those two married?' Ambrosine remarked absently, 'I never knew.'

'I was always led to suppose,' Miss Carey told her gently.

Of all my friends, none drops bricks with greater effect than Ambrosine Phillpotts, for instance: 'What I like about Celia Johnson is that she never does anything common, except, of course, that play you wrote for her.'

To Mrs John Mills, after the marriage of their daughter Hayley, she said, 'I thought John looked marvellous. You must be proud of him. He looked young enough to be your son.'

On seeing a wedding anniversary card on our mantelpiece: 'Your fifteenth wedding anniversary – that's the year the Smith–Bingham marriage went wrong.'

To cheer me up: 'At least you have one friend – I spent the whole afternoon defending you.'

Richard Buckle

AUTHOR, CRITIC AND
EXHIBITION DESIGNER

Gaffes can be covered up by more words, but when your nervous system lets you down physically, recovery is impossible.

I went to a private view at an art gallery carrying a parcel of books. Advancing towards me through the crowd came a charming foreign friend, Princess X, whose name had recently been splashed across the front pages of the papers because she had been accused of walking out of a bookshop with books she had not payed for.

'What have you got in that huge parcel, Dicky?' she asked.

'Books,' I replied. Even that might have been all right, but I *blushed* as I spoke.

Frank Windsor

ACTOR

I once confided in a friend my inability to put a name to faces that I knew and remarked how good Americans seem to be when faced with this dilemma.

'That's because they always announce their names loudly, which encourages me to do the same,' said my friend. 'When this situation next arises, just say loudly, "Frank Windsor".'

Only next morning, walking down Bond Street, I saw approaching me just such a countenance as I'd described to my friend. I waited until he was in hailing distance and then shouted across the pavement, 'Frank Windsor', while pedestrians turned their heads in amazement; he was the only one to reply. 'I'm not Frank Windsor,' he told me and hurried on. I have never tried again.

George Melly

JAZZ SINGER AND WRITER

I had appeared on a TV quiz show in the early 1960s and won an antique rocking-horse. It was very beautiful but without a mane or tail. I was given, however, a bundle of horse hair and eventually found a craftsman able, at a stiff price, to turn it into a hirsute as well as handsome steed.

My wife and I were asked in after dinner to Ken Tynan's. We arrived a little early and joined the table. Among the guests were the lady who directed the TV show and an American film director, known to be a sufferer from total baldness but whose vanity dictated that, not only did he wear a wig, but every morning spent several hours adding eyebrows and lashes one by one. I knew this; my wife did not.

The TV lady asked whether we liked our horse. 'Yes,' said my wife, 'but it was very difficult finding anyone to give it a mane, tail and eyelashes. In the end we found someone but it took hours, every hair had to be inserted one by one, and . . . George, what is the matter? Why are you making those extraordinary faces?'

A typically bizarre account by Mr Melly.

Robin Ray

ENTERTAINER

It is one thing to drop a brick, but what kind of idiot would insist on picking it up only to drop it all over again? This one.

I was about eighteen years old and a very out-of-work young actor. My friend Ronald Harwood was also beginning a career in the theatre and had been lucky enough to get a job in a play called *Malatesta* in which the title role was taken by Donald Wolfit. Ronnie invited me out to Hammersmith to see the play (actors were actually allowed complimentary tickets in those days) and I duly arrived, done up in a grey suit, dark green shirt, red tie, trilby hat and some equally confident opinions.

After the performance I went round to see Ronnie in his dressing room. He introduced me to an attractive girl who had got there just before me – but I wasn't really listening, as I was eager to give my opinion of the performance.

'Well,' said Ronnie, 'what did you think?'

'Oh you were marvellous, of course,' I mused, 'but really someone ought to do something about Wolfit. Strutting round, posturing, up-staging everyone, hogging the limelight. That man is really his own worst enemy!'

Ronnie went a little red and favoured the girl, who was sitting on his left, with a shifty flick of the eyes.

'Yes,' continued the mini George Bernard Agate, 'he needs a firm director like Tyrone Guthrie to prevent him hamming it up.'

Ronnie went redder still. 'Robin,' he said through teeth of glass, 'this is Donald's daughter.'

The following day I was rehearsing a small part in a radio play with members of the BBC Drama Repertory Company. Somehow I just had to exorcize the shameful memory of my blunder, so I turned it into an amusing anecdote against myself. 'It was ghastly,' I concluded to the other actors during coffee-break, 'because Ronnie turned round and said: "This is Donald's daughter!"'

One man laughed even louder than the others. 'Very funny,' he said, 'she's my wife!'

 It is nearly always fatal to try to redeem a brick on the media. Witness the encounter between Ginx Filkender, then at the height of her fame as a New York model, and her interlocutor:

'Tell me, now that your husband is a tennis professional, do you watch him play?'

'Too nervous,' she replied. 'But just before a match I always kiss his balls.'

'We are speaking, of course, of his tennis balls,' remarked the urbane and unfortunate network employee.

Bill Tidy

CARTOONIST

It was the return visit of the North American Cartoonists' Club. They descended on London and I made contact with their advance guard in the offices of *Punch*.

I'd met most of them some time previously in Montreal and scanned the group for familiar faces, the cheerful ones, the twerps, the serious practitioners and the odd-balls. One chap had stuck in my memory: clean, all-American boy, 1947 vintage, with spinning bow tie and a visiting card which actually bore the words 'My Card'. I couldn't spot him and, as my memory for faces isn't too hot, I grabbed the nearest visitor and whispered casually to him, 'Is that twit with the spinning bow tie here?' He smiled and lifted his chin slightly to give his propeller the necessary clearance.

David Sheppard

BISHOP AND FORMER CRICKET
CAPTAIN OF ENGLAND

In 1956 I had been called back into the England Cricket
Team at Manchester against the Australians, who had been
dismissed on the Saturday for 84 runs. On the Sunday I
kept a preaching date at Northampton and after the service
a number of local cricketers came to the vicarage.

'How bad was the wicket?' they asked.

'Certainly not that bad,' I told them. 'An English
County side would have struggled on and made 200 or
250.'

Next morning this remark was splashed all over a
national newspaper. But I was not a popular figure at luncheon: 'I hear you're standing for Parliament next?' one
of the Aussies enquired.

Theo Cowan

PUBLICIST

On the way to a fitting at my tailors, I met the secretary of a client who offered to walk with me to discuss some business matter. We entered the shop deep in conversation and continued talking while I went into a booth to get ready to try on the suit. In a moment of aberration and to the great surprise of the cutter, I presently emerged stark naked.

'Looking for your pyjamas?' my friend asked politely.

Joyce Grenfell

ACTRESS AND AUTHOR

Friends of mine inherited a large, heavy, Victorian house and gradually, room by room, they redecorated the place. At last the dining room was done exactly as they wanted it and to celebrate the completion of the work they gave a dinner party. As the assembled company moved into the new room, one of the guests stopped in the doorway and said, 'Heavens! What fun you'll have doing up *this* room.'

Dickinson

Michael Noakes

ARTIST

Some families can claim a good traditional great-grand-father figure – you know, the type who amassed three fortunes by the time he was twenty-five, but lost each overnight in Drunken Gambling. Or perhaps it was an uncle, the first man ever to introduce moggle-dancing to East Cheam. Alas, the distinctions claimed by my family have been geared more towards resounding clangers; and I fear it is a tendency deeply embedded in my genes.

My father, even as a child, was well advanced as a brick-dropper. Aged eleven, for example, he commemorated his brother's interest in butterflies and moths by buying him, for his thirteenth birthday, what he imagined to be the latest manual for juveniles on Lepidoptera. It was only when the puzzled boy complained that the book was all about having babies that the true subject matter of *The Book for Young Mothers* was established.

In fact, my parents had achieved enough in the direction of making memorable bishes for us all to regard it as quite an amusing family trait – until, that is, the Appleby Incident.

'Michael, why do you say you cannot stand the Applebys?' my mother threw over her shoulder to me from the front seat of the car. Since, at the time, I was sitting next to Dorothy Appleby, also aged sixteen, I did not quite see how to get out of that one.

I tried stammering lack of comprehension, 'Don't know

what you mean . . . Love the Applebys . . . Splendid people . . . charming . . .'

'Nonsense,' said my mother tartly, her mind as firmly on the Appleby track as the car itself, but hideously forgetful that the route had been ordained when we stopped to offer Dorothy a lift home three minutes beforehand. 'Absolute nonsense. Whenever they ask you to tea, you always pretend you've too much homework. Mind you, I can see that the ghastly Dorothy is enough to make even Casanova decide that he has too much homework.'

You can see we have a long and unfortunate history: in fact, it must have taken generations to bring it all to such an unhappy peak in my present family – for I have kept up the tradition. Once, having arranged to meet the painter L. S. Lowry at the side-door of the Tate Gallery – so that I could record a short television interview with him on the occasion of his retrospective exhibition there – I settled the camera-crew in and waited outside on the corner, just in case he forgot the arrangement and went to the front instead. A taxi drew up from the top of the street behind me and Lowry, all umbrella and scarf, scrambled out on to the pavement as a figure darted round from the driver's side to give him some help down the stairs to the side-door. I'll bet he doesn't think to tip that driver, I thought officiously, as I jog-trotted along to them, and felt in my pocket for half-a-crown (as it was then). Drawing level, I greeted my quarry and pressed my tip into the driver's hand – only then realizing that the taxi was drawing merrily away and that the man I had imagined to be the driver, now studying my present in a puzzled manner, was Richard Attenborough.

The thought of exhibitions reminds me of a brief conversation I had on the steps leading to the restaurant of the Royal Academy a couple of years ago. I had submitted a modest picture, hanging at that moment in an obscure part of the galleries, so I really had no grounds for replying in so proprietorial a manner as I did to the comment from a senior Academician whom I passed on the way to a reviving cup of tea. 'Nice exhibition,' he said. 'Thank you!' I replied.

On another occasion connected with my work – I suppose it may have been the stress of the moment that accounted for the curious Spoonerism that I think I heard myself indulge in, in response to a query from a Very Important Sitter when I was painting a portrait at Buckingham Palace. The question was whether I had any brothers. Did I really hear myself reply, 'No, Sam. But I have two misters'?

There are too many minor bricks for comfort ... Turning to see Lowry, the day after that television recording session at the Tate, standing in the next cubicle to me in the men's loo in St Giles's Circus, 'Good Heavens, Mr Lowry!' I said, 'What are you doing here?' ... Or, when greeting a friend at the annual exhibition of the Royal Society of Portrait Painters, I recounted to him the glowing praises of his work that I had overheard a visitor make a little earlier. ' "What command of colour! What mastery of handling! No one in the whole show can touch him," he said.' I ended, 'Anyway it is good to be told these things, so I thought I'd pass it on. Well done ... David.' It was his sudden startled look that replaced his previously happy smile that pulled me up. My use of the wrong name had made it quite clear that I had not just forgotten what he was called – I had cornered the wrong man.

I remember, too, that occasion – not exactly a brick, perhaps, but embarrassing all the same – when I had proudly pointed out my younger son, on the other side of the football pitch during a school match.

'What do you call him?' the other father asked.

I hedged a minute or two.

'All right. So he is six, good at backgammon, keeps three hamsters and wants to be an antique dealer. But what is he *called*?' pursued my relentless interrogator.

'I'm awfully sorry,' I had to admit, 'I'm afraid I've forgotten!'

For Michael
from L.S.L.

George Cole

ACTOR

This is not so much a story of dropping a brick as dropping a door handle. I was appearing in a play in London with Alistair Sim. I had to make a bad-tempered exit, which I did all too well, taking the door handle with me. Alistair Sim was left on stage unable to make his exit shortly after. The set had been established as being on the third floor, so he couldn't use the window. In the end, muttering dreadful oaths directed at me, he left through the chimney!

Driving him home after the show, I was given a severe telling-off. He said I not only broke parts of the set, I broke props, and two of the girls in the play had bruises where I had taken them gently by the arm. He said I must learn to act properly and control my strength. In trying to defend myself I worked too hard again, the car made a terrible noise and I found myself with the gear lever in my hand. I handed it to him and got out and walked home.

Ronnie Barker

COMEDIAN

The brick I most remember dropping was to a man who had been dressing me in a West End play for some five or six months. We were discussing the merits or otherwise of a couple of singers who had appeared on television the night before. He obviously liked them more than I did.

'Well, in my opinion,' said he, helping me on with my jacket, 'they grow on you.' 'Yes – like warts,' said I wittily, and turned around. His face was covered in them.

R. T. Hodder

Two bloomers made by the same headmaster of St Dunstan's I was told, but would not dare assume are true. After hymns and prayers he announced one day to the whole school at assembly that he wished to see Lawrence P. in his study at 10.30.

On another occasion the chapel organ fused and, as repairs would take some time, a father generously agreed to lend the school an electronic instrument. The headmaster announced: 'Chapel *will* take place tomorrow thanks to the generosity of Mr Whitaker, who has agreed to lend us his instrument. However, it is complicated to set up, and I don't want him disturbed. Thus all boys must keep out of chapel between 4.30 and 6.00 today while Mr Whitaker erects his organ.'

Finally an experience with the Wokingham Music Society. After a short recital of pieces three players and myself were keen to go to a pub to recuperate. Our accompanist, Colin Howard, was hopping from one foot to the other, in anticipation of his pint of beer, and surrounded by old ladies saying how much they had enjoyed the concert. 'Yes, splendid, super,' he kept saying to keep them happy. At last a lady appeared brandishing a cheque book: 'I shall have to write the cheque ...'

'Oh, fine, super ...'

'Is that all right?'

'Fine, yes ...'

'Only our treasurer isn't here tonight.'
'Oh, that's okay, fine ...'
'His wife is dying ...'
'Oh, great, marvellous – oh no, I didn't mean it like that.'

Norman Hartnell

THE QUEEN'S COUTURIER

I was lunching one day at a country house when a lull in the conversation left this well-practised designer to compliment my hostess on a silver trophy in the centre of the table.

'I won it for one of my jumpers,' my hostess explained.

'How clever,' I replied. 'Could you knit one for me?'

Auberon Waugh

NOVELIST AND JOURNALIST

Nearly all the worst bricks I have dropped have involved families who have recently suffered a suicide or nervous breakdown among their number, and I do not consider them suitable for repetition.

In a lifetime of dropping bricks, one of the worst and simplest I can remember was when I turned to a lady who had been talking to me unheeded for some time about how much weight she had lost and I asked when she was expecting her happy event.

The worst brick dropped by my father (Evelyn Waugh) was during the war when he met a friend at his club who said he had left his wife behind in Japan just before Pearl Harbor.

'I suppose she has been raped by a hundred Japanese soldiers,' said my father.

'Yes,' he replied.

Janet Suzman

ACTRESS

At that moment when, past someone's left ear, you glimpse a face you know but cannot put a name to, you also know with inexorable timing that The Face will weave its way across to you before you have time to remember. It wove sure enough. Panic.

'Do you know so-and-so?' I cried, waving airily in her direction.

'Don't I just,' hissed The Face. More panic.

He laughed, sort of freezingly I thought, and went for the drinks.

I remembered! Most panic.

I left.

Thus did I, fool that I am, introduce a man to his ex-wife.

Or reintroduce?

Or perhaps, after all, it was the hostess who dropped the bricks?

Edgar Lustgarten

CRIMINOLOGIST

In the Fifties I chaired a BBC radio discussion, honouring a visit to England by Mrs Eleanor Roosevelt. An imposing cast of public figures included Sir David Maxwell Fyfe (afterwards Lord Chancellor as Lord Kilmuir), Lord Boyd and Lady Violet Bonham Carter – and Bertrand Russell. Russell by then had acquired a trick of switching off his majestic intellect and opting out of any social trivia that bored him. Mrs Roosevelt was splendid, every inch the first lady. Before we got to work, I took her round, introducing everyone and she had a friendly talk with each in turn.

When I introduced Russell, she said graciously, 'I cannot tell you what a privilege it is for me to be broadcasting with the world's greatest philosopher.'

Russell stared at her blankly for a moment, then, half-turning away from her said, in a tone of detached indifference: 'What is your name? You sound like an American.'

Bill Grundy

WRITER AND BROADCASTER

Lancashire County Cricket Team were playing the Australians at Old Trafford. Rain – an unusual event in Manchester – had interrupted play, so I scurried for the pavilion. There was the usual pack of members fighting their way to the bar. I fought, too. In the end I won through.

Hacking my way out of the scrimmage I found myself pressed up against a neurologist friend of mine, a man who has been known to tread a grape or two in his time. So I joined his group, which included a solicitor, two doctors, an orthopaedic surgeon, all of whom I'd met before in similar circumstances, and an old gentleman I'd never come across until then. He had the worst case of shakes I'd ever seen. I didn't catch his name as there was too much noise around, but I watched with fascination as he tried to raise his gin and tonic to his lips.

Finally I couldn't resist it: 'Do you drink very much? No, but I spill a lot. I don't wish to know that, kindly leave the stage.' – You know the sort of thing. Then I said, 'Why don't you use your scarf as a sling. Put your right hand in it, pull with your left hand, and that way you'll get the drink to your mouth despite the shakes.'

I suppose it was the general noise in the pavilion that made me unaware of the fact that our group was strangely silent. I was just going to open my mouth again when I received a very sharp kick on the ankle from my neurologist friend. But the old man left in something very like a huff. Only when he'd gone did they tell me that he was one of the finest brain surgeons in the country, that his shake was perpetual, except when he bent over to start an operation, at which time his concentration was such that there was never a trace of the tremor. I've never seen him since. I think he must be avoiding me.

An extrovert after my own heart. Surely only a celebrated interviewer of punk rockers could have waded in deeper.

At my first party political conference, I was at some reception or other and was getting very tired and emotional. I found myself in a corner with a lady I didn't recognize. She seemed to be as relieved as I to have found a spot where we weren't being pushed about. We exchanged civilities and began talking politics. Finally I got on to the Prime Minister of the day – I'm not telling you which – and I began, with a passion inflamed with the water of life I'd drunk, to tell her just how much I detested him, what a closet he was, and so on. She said nothing. I warmed to my task. She said even less. Finally she turned on her heels and left me. Right first time. It was, of course, the Prime Minister's wife.

Not Mr Heath, that leaves Wilson, Douglas Home, Macmillan or Asquith, or, as it was Mr Grundy's first political rally, could it have been Mrs Gladstone?

I was reading the news for Granada TV many years ago. A group of Yorkshire miners had won a lot of money on the football pools and the Editor thought it would be a good idea to bring them across the Pennines to Manchester and let me interview at least one of them as part of the story. A researcher was set to track them down and arrange a car to bring them over. He did it through the local 'stringer', the free-lance reporter who lives locally and knows everybody and everything about his area.

Ten minutes before the news, the miners still hadn't turned up. Frantic phone calls revealed that, yes, they had set out in ample time. The Pennines can be bad in winter so we kept our fingers crossed. Five, four, three, two, one, and I started the news with no sign of my interviewees. Finally, I introduced the piece of film which immediately preceded the pools win story. Immediately, the door of the studio opened and a bewildered miner was thrust at me.

With the Floor Manager telling me there were five seconds to go to the end of the film, I put the victim in his chair, and was suddenly struck with horror. Wasn't there something foreign about his responses? Something definitely un-Yorkshire? And weren't there a lot of Italian immigrants working in the West Riding pits these days? There were. With two seconds to go I asked the man, in Italian, if he spoke English. He shook his head. No. Not a word. I swallowed, turned to the camera, read the news item, altering it as I did so to avoid any reference to the interview.

 It is difficult to understand why he did not continue the conversation, translating as he went along, and earn a nomination for the European Song Contest.

Frank Muir

WRITER AND BROADCASTER

My problem, which at times approaches the speed of paranoia, is remembering names. Not difficult names, which are always poised on the tip of the tongue, but the easy, friendly, much-loved names of friends and colleagues, the forgetting of which becomes a social gaffe of frightful proportions. This, to me, is what the French call – in an old Norman phrase which I have just invented – '*le brick-drop formidable*'.

I have in my time introduced the Director-General of the BBC, to a group anxious to meet him, as the Chairman of the Independent Broadcasting Authority. I have introduced Miss Thora Hird, on television, as 'Miss Hannah Gordon'.

I *know* the name, but when the occasion arises the name simply evaporates. I am rapidly moving towards the terminal '*brick-drop formidable*' as suffered by the late Sir Malcolm Sargent. The story goes – and I pray it is true – that Sir Malcolm, who like Garrick 'dearly loved a lord', once had a member of Scandinavian royalty present at one of his concerts. At the interval he rushed around to the Royal Box with his leading soloist and said proudly, 'Your Majesty, may I introduce Sergio Poliakoff? Sergio – the King of Norway!' The distinguished figure in the box shifted slightly and murmured, 'Sweden'.

Peter Sallis

ACTOR

Straight from the Royal Academy of Dramatic Art, I was awarded the Tennent contract at £12 a week. At my first interview with John Perry and the crowned heads, John Gielgud explained in three minutes how he intended to produce *Richard the Second* and asked what I would like to play. There seemed only one part for me and I opted for the gardener. 'That's cast,' Gielgud told me. Then turning to the others, 'He might be Green, he might be Green!' Then turning back to me he explained kindly, 'We've two men playing Bushy and Baghot, very beautiful, you might make a good contrast.'

Finally cast as Lord Ross or something equally obscure, at the read-through I sat in the rear rank behind Paul Scofield, Joy Parker, Herbert Lomas, Veronica Turnleigh, Richard Wordsworth and all. After the read-through Gielgud offered his congratulations to the cast, adding, 'There's only one voice that is wrong, and that is,' he considers his list, 'Peter Sallis. What are you playing?'

'Lord Ross,' I explained meekly.

'How would you like to play servant to the Duke of York?'

Later he probably had to tell this to John Perry, who must have pointed out that Sallis was being paid £12 a week, a princely sum in those days, and they could get anyone off the street to play servant to the Duke of York for £8. When Gielgud started to set the play and it came to my entrance, I had to utter the immortal line, 'An hour before I came the Duchess died,' and leave the stage.

Gielgud called me back: 'Peter is that all you do?'

'Yes.'

'Oh Christ!'

I finally got to play the gardener, but not in that production, and I only mention it to give the story a happy ending.

Michael Barratt

BROADCASTER AND AUTHOR

Back in 1966, I was interviewing two black politicians from Rhodesia, representing the rival Zapu and Zanu parties. It was a live programme and one of the politicians put forward what seemed to me a specious argument which led me to round on him. 'That's all very well,' I said, 'but two blacks don't make a white.'

Peter Bull

ACTOR

Suppose we start with my father. My mother and he went to meet my future housemaster at Winchester. They weren't mad about him but thought the school was an excellent bet for me. On their return, my father wrote two letters: one to my preparatory school headmaster, giving his candid opinion of Major Blank, and another to the military housemaster saying how much he hoped I would be in his house. My mother, acting as temporary secretary, put the letters in the wrong envelopes – which did not help my career at Winchester get off to a good start.

Milton Goldman, the distinguished American agent, has a habit of introducing everybody to everybody else several times over at parties, which is actually a splendid habit. When Sybil Burton got married to Jordan Christopher he found it very difficult to remember her new name, so before his party he practised all day saying 'Mr and Mrs Jordan Christopher'. Then, at his moment of supreme triumph, having managed to get their names trippingly off his tongue, he led the couple over to Richard Watts of the *Evening Post* and said, 'I want you to meet Richard Burton.'

When Mrs Patrick Campbell finally went to Hollywood, she once sat next to a famous romantic star at a dinner party.

'You're a very handsome young man,' she said, 'You ought to be in pictures.'

'But, Mrs Campbell, I am Joseph Shilderkraut.'

'Well you can always change your name,' retorted Mrs Pat.

Backstage at the American production of *A Bed Before Yesterday*, I met Carol Channing for the first time. We talked together for a while and then she took my hand and, putting it over her heart, she said, 'For years I've been longing to meet you. Your name has been a legend to me, John Bull.'

 We are indebted to Mr Bull, not only for his own bricks, but also to those he has gleaned along the way.

Back to Sir John Gielgud, I'm afraid, who, having experienced Richard Burton's *Hamlet* on a night when he claimed he had a hint of a cold, Sir John said to him, 'I'll come back when you're better ... in health I mean, of course.'

A local Cornish newspaper once carried this review of a play at Perranporth: 'Mr John Penrose gave a sharp twist to both his parts.'

Asked to speak to a women's club at their annual open evening – 'This is a very special evening, we tried to get Arianna Stassinopoulos and we got Peter Bull.'

 What about me and Natalie Delon, asked Mr Bull in his letter, so here is one of my own more horrendous bricks, mentioned in the preface.

While making the film *When Eight Bells Toll*, I had as a leading lady, Natalie Delon, whose husband at that time was the subject of a good deal of adverse publicity in connection with the violent death of his bodyguard. Aware that Miss Delon would be chary of any mention of battle, murder or sudden deaths, I successfully managed to avoid all three subjects until practically the last day of the shooting (*sic*), but then I was suddenly handed a revolver by the director and told to point it at this camera and fire as soon as the latter came in view.

We were at this time in separate motor-boats and Miss Delon was the sole passenger in mine. 'When you fire a revolver, Natalie,' I asked her, 'do you use one hand or two?' And then, turning seawards, started to blush so heavily that I realized the Technicolor print would be quite useless.

Paul Scofield

ACTOR

John Gielgud is, of course, the name that springs to mind in this context, and the only bricks I ever actually heard him drop are decidedly scurrilous and concerned with living victims. But if one is to take him as the prototype brick-dropper, it is perhaps worth observing that really funny bricks are never dropped in malice but in total innocence, which is swiftly succeeded by the dawning realization of the possibility of malicious interpretation. I think the brick-dropper must have some sun too, later. I mean, for instance, when at a dress-rehearsal of his production of a Mozart opera at Covent Garden, something went wrong on stage and Gielgud shouted, 'Oh stop, stop, stop! Do stop that *dreadful* music!' I think he must have enjoyed that one *afterwards*.

This book is in danger of becoming a tribute to Sir John. But has Mr Scofield never dropped a brick himself? However, let us hear from the great man himself.

John Gielgud

ACTOR AND DIRECTOR

When Clement Attlee was Prime Minister, I was asked to meet him at Stratford-upon-Avon at a supper at the Falcon Hotel after he had attended a performance (one I was not in myself). I sat next to his daughter and the conversation turned on where we lived.

'I have a very convenient home in Westminster,' I remarked. 'So easy to walk to the theatre. And where do you live?'

Miss Attlee looked distinctly surprised and replied curtly, 'Number ten, Downing Street.'

 Mmm.

Norman St John-Stevas

MEMBER OF PARLIAMENT, BARRISTER AND AUTHOR

Lord Portarlington was at a reception at which Queen Victoria was present. He went up to her and said, 'Damn it, Ma'am, I know your face but I cannot put a name to it.'

Queen Victoria's reply is, unhappily, not recorded.

 At the risk of capping Norman St John-Stevas's imperturbable locks, I recall a similar tale told to me about Princess Margaret – an encounter with a young man searching valiantly for her identity across a crowded room.

'How are you getting on these days, keeping busy?'

'Fairly,' she told him.

'The old firm still flourishes, eh?'

'You could say that.'

'Your sister still well I hope, still flourishing?'

'Still Queen.'

There was not much left to do but for the poor fellow to walk backwards through the French windows and over the balcony.

Whilst in the political arena, I recall with pleasure the explanation given by a member of the Tory Shadow Cabinet, attempting to burnish his leader's image: 'What people don't understand about Margaret Thatcher is that she will insist on saying what she thinks.' Unfortunately the lady in question was unable to supply us with one of her own.

Tim Brooke-Taylor

WRITER AND ONE OF 'THE GOODIES'

While at Cambridge, a friend of mine – a friend, you understand – had been fixed up with a blind date. Being an optimist, he called at a chemist on the afternoon of the big day and bought himself a packet of contraceptives.

That evening he met his date. He recognized her. She had sold him the contraceptives.

Enoch Powell

MEMBER OF PARLIAMENT

Visiting New Zealand for the first time shortly before the outbreak of war in 1939, I was a guest at the N.Z. Club in Wellington and found myself in agreeable company with some of the members, who were, of course, unknown to me.

There was at that time some difference between the official and the market rate of exchange between Australian and New Zealand pounds; and in the course of the meal I enquired of my affable neighbour where I could get some Australian pounds exchanged at a good rate.

I only understood the sudden cessation of cordial relations with him when, on inquiring after the meal as to his identity, I was told, 'That is the Governor of the Bank of New Zealand.'

Christina Foyle

BOOKSELLER

At one of my literary luncheons, the Duchess of Leinster was sitting next to comedian Jimmy Edwards.

During lunch, she leaned across to me and said in a loud stage whisper, 'A funny thing about Mr Harry Wheatcroft, he can't bear the smell of roses.'

Peter Sellers

ACTOR

In my salad days I struck up an instant romance with a girl I met at a dance and suggested I might be allowed to walk her home. It was such a lovely evening, I suggested we should go home along a bridle path.

'It's far too early in the day to think of getting married, Peter,' was her candid reply.

Cyril Fletcher

COMEDIAN AND WRITER OF ODD ODES

Once at a party, I gave a fellow a blow-by-blow account of the intricacies of Fleet Street finance, instancing how the ever-popular *Evening News* kept the *Daily Mail* financially afloat. I had no idea, of course, that he was Vere Harmsworth.

Norman Plastow

ARCHITECT

A friend of mine, an engineer named Monroe, found himself sitting next to a very plain girl at a rather imposing dinner. Looking desperately around the table for inspiration he came up with the opening remark, 'I see they've seated me next to the goose.' Then realizing what he had said, he added, 'I – I mean the one on the table.'

William Franklyn

ACTOR

The feed line you need to your particular gag, hopefully, comes professionally-timed on the stage, within a gnat's wink of perfection. In life you wait in vain for the feeds until the gag itself has got lost in the 'other trivia' tray! Then, unexpectedly, on blue writing paper, from Robert Morley in up-river Wargrave comes the feed that the starved gag is near dying for. You must decide, dear reader, for yourself whether it is the worst brick or the art of brick-dropping.

Quick setting of the scene: late Georgian cottage being re-furbished on site; maximum three workers, usually one ... Standing by the gate looking at the house ...

A voice, sounding for all the stage world like a comic policeman, mutters humbly in my ear, 'Oh excuse me, sir? I wonder if you could help me?'

My reply floated like a line out of any stage thriller: 'Good morning, Sergeant. I didn't steal the house, but the owners were in a hurry to get rid of it.'

Ignoring the spirit of my flippant interruption, the policeman replied, 'What? Oh yes, sir. Have you a man called Cooper on the site?'

I pointed out that surnames were as unusual in the building trade as Christian names are in the Foreign Office. He took my laboured wit uncomprehendingly. I added that as the site was not a re-build of the Shell-Mex building or an extension of the Barbican, one of *two* (on this day) workers might be Cooper. Deduction had an even chance.

Ted was rounding the corner of the house as I called him. I didn't know much about Ted except that he was quiet, spent lunch in the local betting office, was very willing and not incapable in the building trade. He walked over to the Sergeant and myself, and to save him any introductory offer, I said that the Sergeant was interested in having a word with a man called Cooper.

'It's not your surname is it?' I added vaguely.

'No, my name is Jameson,' he replied.

'I have reason to believe, Mr Jameson, that you are also in fact Mr Cooper,' the Sergeant said, not skirting around any niceties, 'and four weeks ago you were seen entering and leaving a house in Kelso Road that was later found to have been burgled.'

What I hadn't noticed, and neither had 'John Law', was that Ted had an early nineteenth-century brick in his right hand which he dropped with a fast-moving bent elbow on the Sergeant's foot.

It was done with such dexterity that a nerve running up the Sergeant's leg was, for the foreseeable future, inadequate to its task.

It was simple, pure, real-life farce played to perfection, and to a small, particularly unappreciative audience. Ted's particular art of brick-dropping was so literal.

Jeremy Thorpe

FORMER MEMBER OF PARLIAMENT AND LEADER OF THE LIBERAL PARTY

The worst thing that anybody can say to a politician is, 'You won't remember me.' The approach is a form of vanity to discover if one has indeed remembered the questioner. I once made a supreme effort and replied, 'Of course I remember you, you are Miss Bag.'

'No,' came the thunderous reply, 'I am Miss Gas.'

Nigel Nicolson

AUTHOR AND PUBLISHER

It was early June 1940. I was a newly-joined subaltern in the Grenadier Guards, stationed at Wellington Barracks in complete safety and shameful comfort, while most of my brother officers were retreating from Dunkirk. One morning I came down to breakfast in the Officers' Mess, shiny in my new uniform and polished boots, and helped myself to bacon, eggs, sausages and kidneys. The conversation was naturally all about Dunkirk.

'I hear,' I said, 'that the regular troops have been behaving very well. The people who behaved really badly were those who got out first – the gunners and the sappers – who panicked, got drunk, and rushed the boats.'

There was an uneasy silence round the table. I looked up, and saw sitting at the far end of the table two men I hadn't noticed before, a colonel in the Royal Artillery and a captain in the Royal Engineers. Their uniforms were stained with salt water, their faces unshaved and gaunt with sleeplessness and strain. They had just returned from the beaches and were eating their first proper meal for ten days.

After a pause, the colonel simply said, 'It's quite obvious that this young officer wasn't there himself.'

In the circumstances, it was the most charitable remark I have ever heard.

The Printed Brick

MILES KINGTON

Dropping bricks? Good heavens, there's nothing you can teach Fleet Street people about dropping bricks. It's part of their way of life. Whether it takes the form of misquoting, or printing the right gossip about the wrong person, or plain libel, or getting your facts hopelessly wrong, or printing grovelling apologies ... or just good old misprints. Whole books of misprints have been published, all taken from newspapers. The most consistently funny feature in *Punch* is 'Country Life', an anthology of bricks in print, sent in by the readers. The *Guardian* newspaper is famous for its misprints.

Why, there is even a *Guardian* misprint preserved in brass for posterity. Some years ago the El Vino wine bar decided to put up a plaque in honour of Philip Hope-Wallace, its most faithful and probably wittiest habitué. And so, mentioning his eminence as a wit, raconteur and critic, it was duly placed above his usual seat on the wall and unveiled at a small ritual.

'I don't want to seem ungrateful,' said the recipient, peering at it closely, 'but there's only one l in Philip and you've put two.'

'How can that be?' gasped the management. 'We were careful to check with the *Guardian*.'

The first man I worked for as a journalist was John Lawrence, the then Arts Editor of *The Times*, who had started out many years before as a very junior employee of that paper, and there is a well-established story about those days which shows that bricks are nothing new in Fleet Street. A notable peer called, I think, Lord Bessborough died one day and *The Times* duly trundled its stock obituary into print. Unfortunately there was a slight fault of liaison and the obituary printed was of someone with a very similar name.

The next morning an angry phone rang at *The Times*, and John

Lawrence, being the only employee who had bothered to arrive, answered it fearfully.

'Lord Desborough speaking,' said a voice. 'Look here, you've printed my obituary in *The Times* this morning!'

To which, I am glad to say, the young Lawrence reputedly had the wit to say: 'And where are you speaking from now, your Lordship?'

It would be hard to imagine, but bricks can even be dropped with cartoons. For many years the last cartoon in *Punch* was always drawn by an artist called Douglas who did not, like most other cartoonists, send in a preparatory rough but provided the finished drawing and even wrote printers' instructions on it. But the day came when the Art Editor felt that a new Douglas cartoon wasn't good enough and wrote on it the mollifying rejection message 'Sorry – not this one'.

Liaison, however, lapsed again and, instead of the cartoon being sent back to the artist, it found its way to the printer. It duly appeared in *Punch*. The caption? 'Sorry – not this one.' By some miracle, though, it more or less fitted the drawing, which showed two telephone engineers grappling with wires in a hole in the road; it seemed as if one engineer was answering a call (999 perhaps?) and speaking the Art Editor's message down the phone.

It was the literary department's turn to blush when *Punch* received a piece from Larry Adler in New York and, glad to have a famous name in the paper, decided to take the piece even though it was not strictly very good; it was, in fact, very bad and Basil Boothroyd spent much time trimming, rewriting and reshaping it. Eventually it just about passed muster and the immortal mouth organist's name appeared in print.

Another missive appeared from New York almost immediately. 'Glad you used the piece,' gushed Larry Adler. 'I enclose another one. Maybe you would like to know some personal details about me. I am a nineteen-year-old student at Columbia University ...' It was a totally different Larry Adler. Which goes to show that you can drop bricks or have egg on your face without the subject of the brick even knowing about it.

The trouble with dropping bricks in print is that they stay there for all time, unless you go to the lengths of obliterating all the evidence. Or it may even happen that a brick is so glaring that it never gets into print. Sir Philip Gibbs, a veteran journalist of the early twentieth century, was once detailed to cover the opening of the great White City Exhibition by George V and Queen Mary. When he arrived, he was mortified to find that all the journalists present had been herded behind a rope like the common public, even though they were dressed in top hats and tails just like the dignitaries. So that, when the royal party passed, Gibbs could not resist the temptation to skip over the rope and join the royals, especially as one member of the party, a French Cabinet Minister, had failed to arrive and the Equerry who then counted heads failed to notice the new arrival.

Keeping very casually to the back of the party, Gibbs found himself next to Queen Alexandra, the then Queen Mother, who was very deaf and kept to herself on such occasions. But finding someone else at a loss, she joined Gibbs in the perambulation and he found himself having to provide a lot of small talk, none of which she could hear. As soon as he could, Gibbs left to file his very first-hand report, but when he returned to his newspaper, he found the Picture Editor most upset. 'I have all these lovely photographs of the royal party, Gibbs,' he stormed, 'and I can't use them because *you* are in all of them!'

Not so lucky was the young man who reviewed jazz in the 1960s for, I believe, the *Daily Telegraph* without knowing much about it. He once reviewed a record by the fine jazz pianist Teddy Wilson who was described on the back of the sleeve as having a 'trumpet-style approach'. Not bothering to listen to the record itself, he wrote at length about Teddy Wilson's fine trumpet playing. There was no trumpeter on the record. He eventually came to grief when he reviewed a jazz concert a little in advance of the day of the performance. He sent in the piece on the right day and it was printed; the concert however was cancelled. The reviewer was cancelled thereafter too.

Such things may happen even to the most knowledgeable of critics. Richard Williams, now editor of *Time Out*, is an expert on advanced jazz and rock music, so was given the job ten years ago of dealing with a new John Lennon LP. One side, reported Williams, was devoted to fairly conventional songs, but the other side was *very* experimental. It contained an electronic tone which continued throughout the whole side, varying slightly from time to time, giving a fascinating glimpse of the *avant-garde* side of John Lennon and his interest in electronic music. Or so Williams wrote. In fact, the noise he was reviewing so seriously was merely an endless tone placed there by the engineers to indicate that there was no music at all on the second side. It was a long time before his cynical colleagues let Richard forget that gaffe.

A colleague of mine was asked last year if he would put together a book of Fleet Street stories. I have no doubt that almost all Fleet Street stories would deal with goofs and gaffes. I also have no doubt that it would be impossible to gather the best ones into one volume, which is probably why my colleague wisely declined to edit the book. If anyone should have done it, that man was Vincent Mulchrone who, until his lamented death in 1977, told the best (alas, now uncollected) stories about Fleet Street that I have heard. But one story that he might not have included, because it was about himself and he was a modest man, concerned the time he got drunk on a train he wasn't on.

Vincent was due home one evening to go to a social occasion for which it was very important that he should not be late or, as sometimes happens to journalists, with a few drinks inside him. He promised his wife faithfully that he would be abstemious and punctual. He even promised that, to make sure, he would travel on an early train which had no buffet car. Not only that, he even got on the train in question and set off from Waterloo with a clear conscience.

Three hundred yards out of Waterloo the train stopped. It stopped for a long time. Vincent sat in his compartment without a drink and even without a cigarette, with the train showing no signs of starting again. The only thing that happened to relieve the monotony was that a train going *into* Waterloo drew up opposite him and started an equally long vigil. And, he suddenly realized, the carriage that had stopped right by his window was the buffet car. Buffet car! Cigarettes!

After some fiddling through the windows with change and little packets and boxes of matches, Vincent secured a smoke. Then another thought occurred to him: surely it would not be too difficult to get just a little Scotch from the other train? He made motions at the passengers in the buffet. They understood. Money changed hands and a Scotch came through. Later, another. After that, just one more. Then one more for the rail.

When Vincent finally emerged at his home station, he was a little unsteady on his legs. His wife noticed immediately.

'Oh, Vincent! You *have* been drinking!'

'No, dear, I haven't. It's just that ...'

But how can you explain that you haven't dropped a brick when the true explanation sounds even worse?

Lew Grade

IMPRESARIO

When I was an agent and went to the theatre – the old Metropolitan in the Edgware Road – I once saw an act there called Winters and Fielding, which I thought was great. I rushed round to them backstage and told them how terrific they were and how I would make them stars if I handled them, would get them big salaries, much better than their present agencies.

When I had finished speaking, I said, 'By the way, who are your agents?'

They replied, 'Lew and Leslie Grade.'

Another brick was dropped by Ivor Spencer, the toastmaster. At a big reception he introduced my wife Kathie and I as 'Sir Lew and Leslie Grade'.

Richard Marsh

CHAIRMAN OF THE NEWSPAPER
PUBLISHERS' ASSOCIATION

The only major social gaffe I can remember was an occasion when I mistook a lady at a party for the wife of one of my colleagues. I walked up to her and, with heavy humour, said brightly, 'Are you still living with that dreadful man Jones?'

She turned her back on me angrily and one of my other colleagues explained gently that she was not the wife of the man I thought she was, but has, in fact, been having an affair with him for some years.

Fanny Cradock

COOKERY AUTHOR AND BROADCASTER

With unerring instinct, Robert, you have picked on a prime brick-dropper who began at the early age of six weeks by being violently sick over her most wealthy and influential godmother. I went from bad to bloody horrible, via a clanger which can still make my cheeks burn when I remember it.

The scene: Thunder Hall in Herts. Me: a sub-deb at her first house-party. During dinner my future aunt by marriage, very elderly even then, said solicitously across the table, 'We do hope, dear, that you will not find us inordinately dull. I fear we live a very quiet life.'

To which I replied cheerfully, 'I am sure I shall not – I am very easily amused.'

I have precedent. My Mama dropped a brick, when she was the same age, which is much quoted even today. Her mother, my beloved Gran, was giving a luncheon party. My Mum was allowed 'down', but naturally was placed well below the salt at this 'pink' luncheon for some twenty people. She adored my Grandfather, who was everlastingly in trouble with Gran through his monstrous vulgarity in 'collecting' fine porcelain. By Gran's book it was either inherited or 'struck' because royalty were coming to stay. Grandfather had no such inhibitions and Spinks knew him well.

As desert was served, Mum noticed that Grandfather was talking very earnestly to a large VIP woman on his right. She caught the word 'Sèvres' and feared the worst. Sure enough, when Grandpa had removed the dessert forks from his plate and set aside his finger bowl, he turned the plate over and was clearly peering at the mark. Into the breach rushed Mum, saying rather shrilly, 'Oh, pray do not worry, Lady Mandeville. Why you know, if my father thought you were valuable, he would turn you up and see if you were marked.'

Bernard Delfont

IMPRESARIO

Once, at a dinner I was attending, the function Chairman was asked by a guest, following the Loyal Toast, if he could smoke. To which the Chairman responded: 'Of course you may – the Queen is drunk.'

André Previn

COMPOSER AND CONDUCTOR

Anyone engaged in the performing arts seems to have a genius for dropping the most appalling bricks, and my contributions to the total have been regular. Therefore, instead of racking my brain for the single most horrendous one, I will simply recount the latest instance.

After a rehearsal with the London Symphony Orchestra, I was sitting in the bar of the Westbury Hotel, having a drink with our soloist of the day. I looked up and saw a young American composer whose work I had admired come into the room and look around for a friendly face. I beckoned him over and ordered him a drink.

He settled down happily and made polite enquiries about the forthcoming concert. 'I heard your orchestra a few nights ago,' he continued. 'It sounded absolutely marvellous. It was the night the Beethoven Sixth was played in the first half.'

I thanked him and then had a sudden recollection of that particular evening. 'Oh God,' I said, 'that was the night Pollini was supposed to play the Fourth Piano Concerto in the second half, and he cancelled, and we were stuck with one of those last-minute substitutions, that really appalling, third-rate lady pianist. I'm really sorry you had to suffer through that.'

The young composer gave me a long and thoughtful look. 'That's all right,' he said coolly, 'I didn't mind. The pianist is my wife.'

Stuart Burge

THEATRE DIRECTOR

At the first night of *Once A Catholic* the theatre's Board and the guest of honour were on this occasion joined in the front row by someone hastily introduced as Tennessee Williams. In the interval, suitably impressed, the distinguished strangers crowded into the little office and proceeded, over the drinks, to compliment such a distinguished dramatic author who, for once, seemed strangely reticent and apparently unable to remember the titles of his plays.

Finally Norman St John-Stevas, jogging his drink and his memory, said, 'Tennessee, you can't have forgotten the time I found you wandering round the West End the worse for wear and took you home in my Rolls Royce?'

The recipient of so gracious a comment confessed his bewilderment, 'I don't know who you think I am, but my name is George Tennessee and I'm a bandleader.' The bell summoning them back to the auditorium did not come one moment too soon.

When John Gielgud was visiting Nottingham in *Veterans* by Charles Wood, he used sometimes to frequent the stalls during my production of *The Tempest* starring Hugh Griffiths. Sir John was troubled at the time by a somewhat hostile reaction to his own play, so I decided to ask him to a supper party, also inviting Hugh Griffiths along. The subject of *The Tempest* came up and Sir John kept everyone, or nearly everyone, amused by his comments on previous productions he had witnessed. Apparently he had not been impressed by the Prospero and he held forth for some time as to the hopeless performance of Caliban in the same production. 'Quite the worst Caliban I have ever seen,' he said. Then glancing at Hugh Griffiths at the other end of the table, 'You're very silent, Hugh.'

'Not as a rule,' said Hugh. 'I was just trying to recall my performance and wondering if you could possibly be right.'

 Any mention of Sir John's name in this context is entirely fictitious!

Lady Shrewsbury

The late King Edward VII, accepting an invitation to a shoot, stipulated that the guests at luncheon should be restricted to the guns and their ladies. His hostess was, however, unable to resist adding considerably to the party.

'I see,' the monarch told her, surveying the assembled company as the footmen opened the hampers, 'that you have invited the *monde*.'

'Only the *demi-monde*, Majesty,' his unfortunate hostess blurted out.

The story was repeated later by my grandmother at a similar picnic, until half-way through the telling she remembered, with icy foreboding, that she now was the guest of the same hostess.

 Did she, I wonder, like the film-maker in Mr Ayckbourn's story abandon the anecdote, or were the Edwardians made of sterner stuff?

Gaia Servadio

ITALIAN JOURNALIST AND AUTHOR

Last summer I was co-chairing a luncheon given by the Foreign Press Association in honour of heads of state for the Commonwealth Summit. I was on my own when the Singapore delegation arrived and my hand went out with a confident smile towards the first man, whose almond-shaped eyes suggested he came from Singapore.

'We are pleased you could come, Prime Minister,' I told him.

'Me,' said the man confused, 'me bodyguard.'

The next man, smartly dressed in a blue suit and too thin to be a bodyguard surely, followed – another silly smile from me, I bowed, 'Thank you for coming to this luncheon, Sir.'

'Me, gorilla of Prime Minister.' He did not shake my hand and settled in a corner of the hall.

Now three other putative Singapore Prime Ministers approached, all in dark blue. I shook hands with all three, but dropped the 'Sir' and the bow. They were not pleased that I had brought attention to their entry – they were all bodyguards.

Suddenly another group of Singapore-looking smartly-dressed men turned the corner and advanced. I did not even smile as they passed me. I was right, or very nearly; nine were bodyguards, but the tenth, alas, was the Prime Minister.

Later, someone else had to pick up the brick.

Margaret Drabble

NOVELIST AND BIOGRAPHER

I love the aplomb of people who deal with them well –
like a friend who recently replied, when a guest of mine
asked after his parents, 'Well my father's dead, so *he's* all
right.'

I think the worst situations are when I find myself airing
my views to an undetected expert – I have lectured the
Editor of the *Observer* on journalism, a Managing Director
of Penguins on publishing Penguins, a lover on his
beloved's performance in the theatre, and I have a nasty
feeling that I once voiced some opinions on modern painting (a dangerous thing to do in any circumstances) to
Ralph Kitaj, who was masquerading at the time as a fellow
parent at a PTA meeting.

Somebody once asked me at a party whether I liked
Margaret Drabble's novels. I bet I have done the same kind
of thing to other people and *don't even know it* to this day.

I think we should all go round with labels on declaring
our names, relationships and affiliations to avoid this kind
of blunder. Occasionally one does try to make warning
noises of forbidden topics to guests, but it always goes
wrong – if one alerts people to the dangers of talking about
such controversial themes as cholesterol, public schools,
natural childbirth, or the reputation of successful fellow
novelists such as John Fowles, John le Carré, Iris Murdoch,
etc., the conversation inevitably goes straight in for the
kill.

There are no answers to these problems. It is safer to give up social life altogether.

Margot Fonteyn

PRIMA BALLERINA

I think we all drop bricks at one time or another; as my husband says, quoting an old Panamanian proverb, 'Even the best monkey can drop a coconut.'

In my opinion the real art of dropping bricks lies in knowing how to retrieve them.

 And here the great ballerina leaves us, as always, asking for more.

Peggy Ashcroft

ACTRESS

No memorable brick dropped by me, but an unforgettable one dropped on me.

John Gielgud, after his first ever production, *Romeo and Juliet*, for the Oxford University Dramatic Society in 1932 – in his curtain speech, holding Edith Evans and myself by the hand, said, 'I hope never to have two such leading ladies again.' (But he did and often.)

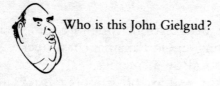

Who is this John Gielgud?

Wendy Toye

DIRECTOR AND CHOREOGRAPHER

The director of a well-known repertory theatre rang a friend of mine and asked if he could, at very short notice, take part in the next production.

The actor said that, unfortunately, he was not free, to which the director replied, 'Oh dear, what a pity! Can you possibly suggest anyone else for the part? I really have scraped the barrel.'

Victor Sassie

RESTAURATEUR

A well-known peer ordered a dinner party for four Chinese diplomats and six distinguished Britons in honour of His Excellency the Chinese Ambassador.

The host told me it was unusual for His Excellency to dine outside his residence, but when he did, he was known never to partake of any food.

The first course was chilled wild cherry soup. I asked, through the aide, would His Excellency test the temperature by tasting? He polished off the lot whilst nodding approval.

At the conclusion of the evening the interpreter called me over and whispered, 'His Excellency asks me to tell you that in having to attend many functions, he has to guard against eating to avoid being gross, but he has a weakness for cherries, and your food contained some of his favourite ingredients like white capsicums. Thank you for an excellent dinner.'

I whispered in reply, 'Please tell His Excellency, I am most grateful and happy to have found a chink in the armour.'

Richard L. Coe

AMERICAN DRAMA CRITIC

As one of those starstruck juveniles for whom a half-century later I feel embarrassed but understanding kinship, I was eleven when I took to playing hookey so I could sneak into Broadway musicals. Sneak is the word. Blessed with theatre-going parents, I was hit early by the thought that if I remembered the precise time of the interval, I might later wander back and glide into a seat for the rarely sold-out midweek matinées.

Getting away from school for a non-existent dental appointment and inspired by a passion for Miss Gertrude Lawrence in the Gershwins' *Treasure Girl*, I decided during my second return to its second act that maybe someone 'back there' might be astonished to see a properly dressed Cathedral of St John the Divine choirboy – hard collar, purple tie and knee pants, an English tradition imported to the Episcopal Diocese of New York. For whatever reason, the stage doorman and her maid did allow me to wait for Miss Lawrence in a flower-crammed sitting room, while someone they called 'the Captain' visited her in an inner sanctum.

I was staggered to hear my beloved's voice refuse to marry whomever it was. After their lingering farewell, she swept into the sitting room, chatted, gave me her picture and autographed it in a grand, angular hand, which subsequently I made sure that everyone who drifted by my cubicle could not miss.

Ten years later I was on the *Washington Post*, assigned to interview Miss Lawrence in her dressing room at Washington's National Theatre. Entering the presence, I still felt like the choirboy in knee pants, though I sported a moustache and enough Washington awareness to recognize the three men in her dressing room: Douglas Fairbanks Jr, Bruce Cabot and Elliott Roosevelt, blond catnip of President Roosevelt's four sons. It was a pride of males a young princess might envy and Miss Lawrence was playing a princess years younger than herself, spreading her glittering charm evenly to each of the trio.

I gasped out: 'Oh, Miss Lawrence, you were so good to me when I was a boy ...'

She looked at me, speechless. 'I think I'd better go,' I said.

'Yes,' she said.

Jilly Cooper

NOVELIST AND JOURNALIST

My husband Leo was giving a very, very distinguished publishing party to launch a spoof military history. The party bristled with celebrities including Osbert Lancaster, who had illustrated the book. One of the important guests of honour was to be Lady Diana Cooper and I was scheduled to wait at the door and, when she arrived, to look after her.

Eventually she arrived looking absolutely ravishing. I gathered her up and took her round, and I introduced her to everybody and said, 'This is Lady Diana, I don't know whether you have met.' And she nodded and smiled, and looked terribly happy and pleased and honoured to be having such a nice time, and everybody was falling over her and was absolutely mad about her, and finally I took her over to introduce her to Osbert Lancaster. I said, 'Osbert, you must know Lady Diana, you must have had many happy romps in the past at parties when everybody was being very grand in the twenties,' and Osbert looked very, very startled and said, yes, of course he knew her, and shook hands with her very gravely and was very polite to her and they had a nice little chat and she was having an absolutely marvellous time and talking to him, when suddenly I went cold inside, because straight through the door came the right Lady Diana. I had been hawking round to all these people, who knew perfectly well it wasn't her, the wife of the War Office librarian.

Humphrey Lyttelton

BANDLEADER AND JOURNALIST

Most bricks are dropped at moments of acute desperation, when the brain slips into neutral and the tongue into top gear.

A year or two ago I attended a family gathering. I should explain here that my great-grandfather sired twelve children by his first wife and, when she died, he married again and had four more. All the children followed his example with the result that, if I wished to trace my family connections, it would be quicker to list those people who are *not* related to me.

Relatives close and distant converged on the family party and I was at a disadvantage from the start since, thanks to the modest notoriety that I have achieved, most of them knew me even though I had lost touch with them. It wasn't simply a matter of putting names to faces – I had to fix them in generations too. Was that handsome and seemingly well-preserved lady in the corner an aunt, a cousin or (goodness, how time flies!) a niece?

For an hour or so I battled manfully, but it was inevitable that I should crack sooner or later. A familiar face loomed from the crowd.

'Hello!' I cried in that crowing voice that one assumes on these occasions. 'The last time I saw you was at your parents' wedding!'

In a voice frosty enough to crack windows, she said, 'I think you mean my brother's.'

The following five bricks were the prize-winners in our public competition mentioned in my Preface.

Dr D. Double

Location: A plant-ridden Belgravia flat decorated with rubber plants and Crotons.

One of the guests, on accepting a banana by way of a little light refreshment, remarked that he never knew what to do with the skin afterwards.

His hostess assured him: 'Oh, do what my husband does. He rolls it up and tucks it behind his scrotum.'

Mrs S. Wise

My husband had to call on a local dignitary. On arrival, he went to the door only to be confronted by a dog, growling and snapping at his heels. As he was trying to decide what to do, a voice from inside called, 'Kick his balls.' My husband looked at the dog and shouted back, 'I can't, it's the wrong way round!'

Whereupon the voice from inside corrected him: 'Not those, you fool, the cricket balls on the lawn.'

Alison Walsh

While on the way home from a holiday in Devon, my sister and I went into a rather exclusive pottery studio to look around. Everything was immaculately set out and there was the cloistered calm associated with an amateur kiln. As we wandered around, keeping our elbows and any other prominent features tucked in for fear of knocking some valuable work of art off the shelves, we were watched by the potter himself, who obviously thought we were about to slip a casserole dish up our jumpers and walk out with it.

Suddenly an interesting object caught my eye – it was a little pot with a long, straight handle sticking out.

My sister, 'What do you think it is?'

Thinking that it might be used for measuring out spirits, I picked it up and, putting on a somewhat upper-class accent, I shattered the silence with: 'Anyone for randy or bum?'

E. K. Whitehead

A few years ago when I was in the USSR, I was staying at a large hotel in Leningrad after visiting a local factory. There were seven lifts in the hotel but only one was working, the one on the extreme right.

I called it on the ninth floor and, when the door slid back, I was confronted by a very tall man who was wearing a huge sombrero made of woven raffia. Perhaps, I thought, he is wearing it so that his wife might more easily recognize him in the milling mob in the foyer, but he was so tall and of such striking appearance that the headgear was really unnecessary. He reminded me of Pooh-Bah – a 'particularly haughty and exclusive person'.

After he had noticed my interest in his headgear, he bent down, touched his sombrero and whispered in my ear, 'The food in the restaurant is bloody awful so I've brought this to eat.'

I agreed with him about the poor quality of the food and he said, 'Would you like a nibble on the quiet?'

I replied, 'Who do you think I am? Guy Burgess?'

And he said, 'I know you are not Guy Burgess, because I am Kim Philby.'

Michael H. Scott

Some years ago, at the time of De Gaulle's retirement, Dorothy and Harold Macmillan were lunching with General and Madame De Gaulle in Paris.

Dorothy Macmillan, after expressing admiration for the achievements of De Gaulle, asked Madame De Gaulle, 'What are you looking forward to now?'

Madame De Gaulle, in a clear and penetrating voice, replied: 'A penis.'

A certain *frisson* went round the table. De Gaulle broke the embarrassed silence by saying: 'My dear, I think the English don't pronounce the word quite like that. It's not "a penis" but " 'appiness".'

Daphne du Maurier

NOVELIST, BIOGRAPHER AND PLAYWRIGHT

My late husband, then Lt-Colonel F. A. M. Browning, DSO, commanding the 2nd Battalion Grenadier Guards stationed in Alexandria, and myself were invited to a luncheon party given by the British Consul.

Social gatherings have never been my favourite sport, but I was determined to be on my best behaviour and not let my husband down.

Cocktails were succeeded by lunch and, as always, I didn't catch the names of the guests on either side of me at the table. Polite conversation passed, and midway through the meal my right-hand neighbour asked what I thought of the political situation and the meeting between Hitler and Mussolini.

'Well they're obviously cooking something up between them,' I replied, 'what with Musso having conquered Abyssinia and having the King of Italy crowned in Addis Ababa. But Musso is such a buffoon, I can't believe he and his black-shirts can do anything frightful. As for Hitler, he really is a menace. Frightful little man, up to no good at all. That greasy hair and awful moustache. I can't think what the German people see in him. But since they lost the war, I suppose any sort of leader is better than none.'

My neighbour made no comment. Silence was profound. He then turned to the guest on his right and did not speak to me again throughout the meal.

After lunch I enquired of someone who he was. 'Oh, the German Chargé d'Affaires,' I was told.

Brian Aldiss

WRITER

My earliest brick

MOTHER (turning round from sink and glaring at me as I sat on the floor): '*What* was that you said?'
SELF (terrified but not entirely losing presence of mind): 'Butter.'

John Braine

NOVELIST AND PLAYWRIGHT

I'm sure that I've dropped hundreds, since I'm loud-mouthed, stupid and totally inconsiderate. I'm sure that I've crashed through life dropping bricks upon every corn in sight. To know me is not to love me. I put the best of myself into my work and there's not much left over for ordinary living.

I do have a very good memory. Why doesn't it function in this area? The answer is that I avoid anything likely to cause me the least discomfort. If I remembered dropping a brick, it would make me uncomfortable. So my memory has a 'wipe' button like a tape-recorder. It does, however, record the very few wise and witty remarks which I've made. I suspect that it adds to them, that when I look back I authentically said what I now wish I'd said. My memory is not only a censor, it's also extremely creative, presenting me always in a good light.

Me, drop a brick? Resoundingly the answer is *never, not ever*. I know that this is some kind of record, that it makes me absolutely unique. But there it is. I cannot contradict my supremely efficient memory.

John Braine turned out to be something of a disappointment, but I include his contribution as an example of someone who, when (as is often the case) he puts his foot down, is pretty confident of where he is standing.

John Schlesinger

FILM DIRECTOR

As a child I had a wonderful knack of emptying a railway carriage by pulling my sweater over the top of my head so that people thought I was headless, or by assuming the most frightful tic. My convulsions would invariably prevent anyone from entering the compartment, and thus I had it to myself and friends or family.

Only a few years ago I was planning to spend the weekend in the country with an American friend of mine. We had not seen each other for a long time, and met at Charing Cross Station. We decided to avoid the rush-hour and take a later evening train.

We sat facing each other in an empty compartment with a great deal to talk about, earnestly hoping that no one would join us. I suggested the perfect remedy, remembering what had succeeded forty years ago, and started up a tic so grossly overplayed that I felt sure no one could possibly risk entering the compartment. Every time a late-departing business man peered into the carriage, he went in search of another. So far so good, we thought. By this time, my American friend was fairly hysterical, so I had a good audience.

A moment before departure, a bowler-hatted city gent, clutching an evening paper, opened the door catching me, so to speak, in 'mid-tic'. I thought I had better keep it up as he slammed the door shut with his elbow, sat down opposite us and opened his paper with his right arm, on the end of which was a metal hook. Difficult moment of decision. Obviously we were caught red-handed and I was far too embarrassed to continue the act, but we were both helpless with laughter and, as prisoners of the train until Tunbridge Wells, we kept having to invent imaginary things that had amused us during the day, so that we did not further embarrass our unfortunate neighbour.

If this particular city gent reads this, I hope he will forgive us and understand that we were not laughing at his affliction, but at a situation which had totally misfired.

Cecil Beaton

PHOTOGRAPHER AND DESIGNER

A man called on Sir John Gielgud in his dressing-room at the theatre to congratulate him on his performance.

Sir John said, 'How pleased I am to meet you. I used to know your son, we were at school together.'

The man replied, 'I have no son, I was at school with you.'

Michael Frayn

PLAYWRIGHT

Most of the bricks I've dropped in the course of my life seem to have landed on my own toes (unless I've simply failed to notice the spasms of pain passing across other people's faces). I still get a noticeable twinge when I recall my first entry into the world of the theatre.

This was nothing to do with writing plays (that came many bruised toes later). It was when I was a reporter on the *Manchester Guardian*; I was about twenty-four years old – it was my first job. I hadn't the slightest interest in plays at that time, either in writing them or even in watching them. All I cared about was reviewing them, because that was one of the jobs you had to do if you worked in the *Guardian* Reporters' Room in those days. We covered the local reps and amateur dramatic societies as far out as Sheffield and Liverpool. If you wrote your notice of a play at the Liverpool Shakespeare during the last act, turning half-round in your seat and holding up a pad of copy-paper to catch the light from the stage, you could just manage to phone your copy through afterwards and get the last train back to Manchester. I had dreams of being a proper London reviewer – not because I wanted to see the plays in London, or even to meet actresses, but because I would be hobnobbing with all the great men who reviewed for the national papers in such a dazzling blaze of witticisms and by-lines. I might even find myself speaking to Ken Tynan, whose reviews in the *Observer* at that time seemed to me probably the main reason why God had invented Sunday.

Well, one day my chance came: I was sent to review a play in Bristol. On the long train journey south (it took all day, as I recall) I grew more and more excited. It was the first night of a new play at the Bristol Old Vic, they'd all be coming! The play had won a prize in an *Observer* competition, so Tynan himself was bound to be there! As the stalls filled up, and the buzzing tension of a first-night audience thickened in the air, I twisted back and forth in my seat, craning my neck in every direction, shamelessly star-spotting. The man sitting next to me took out a pencil – he was obviously the critic from the local paper. Thinking he would be feeling the same provincial and professional excitement as myself, I leaned sideways and shared my anxiety with him. 'Can't see Tynan anywhere!' I twittered.

At that moment the house-lights went down, the curtain rose, and I resigned myself to sitting through Act One before I could resume my evening's entertainment. But then I became aware that the man with the pencil had turned and was staring at me oddly in the darkness. A terrible suspicion came to me, hardening slowly into certainty as the play unreeled in front of my unseeing eyes.

I wrote a savage notice. I never became a London reviewer. And whenever I've met Tynan since I've found it difficult to forgive him the blinding embarrassment I caused myself.

Osbert Lancaster

CARTOONIST, ARTIST AND AUTHOR

During the war I was in the Foreign Office; returning on the boat-train from France and sharing the carriage was someone who looked vaguely familiar talking French to a companion. Anxious to prove that I never forgot a face or a fellow diplomat, I chatted away to him happily, interspersing many *chèrs collègues* into the conversation, when it suddenly dawned on me that this particular Frenchman was not engaged in high affairs of state but currently running The Ivy restaurant and I had just enough presence of mind to change the topic of conversation to whale steaks.

Then I was fortunate enough to be present at the event of Tom Driberg's fortieth birthday party in the House of Commons. Among the guests was the new and shiningly Caucasian wife of Sir Seretse Khama of Botswana. It was Kingsley Martin, then editor of the *New Statesman*, who dropped the best brick I ever heard:

'Well, my dear,' he told her affectionately, 'you're the nigger in this woodpile.'

Antonia Fraser

BIOGRAPHER AND MYSTERY WRITER

During a very bad fog in 1967 my then husband, Hugh Fraser, and I went to dinner with Nigel Lawson and his wife in Chelsea. Conversation was dominated by the topic of the fog, and most people left quite early to get back to Belgravia, Kensington or, in our case, Campden Hill. Except, that is, one poor little man who seemed rather down on his luck, not surprisingly as he lived somewhere in Surrey and all the evening trains had been cancelled.

I said kindly, 'Come back and spend the night with us ...'

I couldn't remember his name, but he seemed nice enough, though down-trodden. Showing him to a bed, I asked him where he wanted to get to in the morning.

'Near Whitehall,' he replied.

'Well, you're in luck,' said I. 'My husband happens to be a Government Minister and he will give you a nice ride down to Whitehall in his lovely big car. I bet you have never done that before. So, you see, your evening has not turned out badly after all.'

He vanished before I was up in the morning. In the evening, I said to my husband, 'Was that poor fellow OK? I bet he enjoyed the ride in the official car, fog or no fog.'

'Yes. He was OK,' replied my husband, 'but I don't think the ride in the official car was quite such a treat for him as all that. You see, after all, Sir William Armstrong *is* the Head of the Civil Service.'

Joan Bakewell

WRITER AND BROADCASTER

It wasn't so much a brick that was dropped as a skirt that was raised.

It was an afternoon charity affair at which I was compering a gala entertainment of very distinguished performers: they ranged from a famous television magician to stars from Covent Garden. It was not in a theatre but in rather a distinguished setting adapted for the occasion. This meant that a fairly low platform edged with festoons of foliage had to serve as a stage.

Our distinguished guest – (not She, but one of The Family) – attended our proceedings with the utmost charm. She (there's another clue) sat and talked with many of those for whom the entertainment had been planned. As the occasion drew to a close, she came forward and reached up to borrow from me the stand microphone I had been using to give an impromptu word of greeting and thanks to everyone. I lifted the tall microphone down to Her. The chattering hall grew quiet and attentive. She spoke – then moved to hand the microphone back to me. Rather than trouble Her with the struggle of cable wires, I grasped it quickly and heaved it back towards the stage. As I lifted, I failed to notice that the splayed feet at the base of the microphone had become entangled and were slowly but steadily lifting the royal skirt. I pulled still higher; only then did a beaming smile draw my attention to the mishap. Modesty was saved just in time.

Tantalizing. Could it have been the Queen Mother, Princess Anne or, a trifle more prosaically, the Duchess of Gloucester? What goes up must come down. For the reverse of this story see Desmond Morris's essay.

Simon Gray

NOVELIST, PLAYWRIGHT AND LECTURER

I once informed the Master of a Cambridge College, whom I did not recognize, that the lady with whom I had just conversed was a ghastly old woman. He courteously identified her for me as his wife. Five minutes later I told this as an amusing anecdote to a new man who revealed himself as their son.

Sewell Stokes

AUTHOR

In the days of my youth, at a friend's house in the South of France, I met Somerset Maugham for the first time. When, a week later, he graciously accepted my invitation to lunch, I was particularly anxious to make a favourable impression on him, in the hope that he would allow me to take advantage of the occasion by interviewing him for an American magazine to which I contributed pen-portraits of English celebrities. Among topics we discussed over lunch was the regrettable habit film directors then had of altering the plot of a novel to suit themselves, to the extent even of changing a sad ending into a happy one. And I was able to cite a case in point, having the previous day discussed this heinous practice with none other than Rex Ingram.

Mr Ingram was a director famous at that time for his productions of *The Four Horsemen of the Apocalypse* with Rudolf Valentino and *The Prisoner of Zenda* with Ramon Navarro. He was at present filming, in Nice, a novel about a sinister magician that he had bought for no better reason than its suitability as a starring vehicle for an actor he had under contract.

'The story is no good whatever,' Ingram said, 'just a melodramatic plot ending in the death of the heroine. But I've given it a happy ending. It was the only thing to do.'

I mentioned something about happy endings being a trifle banal.

'Oh I entirely agree,' Ingram was quick to say. 'But then you need a first-rate story, a work of some merit to justify an unhappy climax. When filming a serious piece of fiction I naturally stick to the end as it is written. But with cheap melodrama like the one I am directing now, how one alters it couldn't matter less.'

Repeating the director's caustic words I was ignorant of the fact that I'd have done better to leave them unsaid.

Somewhat coldly, Mr Maugham said: 'In point of fact, I don't consider *The Magician* to be one of my better works.'

Grania ffrench Blake

A Hungarian diplomat, making a speech at a rather pompous embassy party, said, 'I am not wanting to make too long speech tonight as I am knowing your old English saying, "Early to bed and up with the cock".'

Richard Gordon

AUTHOR OF THE 'DOCTOR' SERIES

When I was a medical student, I hated *viva voce* exams. I hated facing my pair of inquisitors eyeball to eyeball, aware that I might be wearing the wrong tie or expression. 'Go to table C,' whispered the porter in my gynaecology finals, to my relief indicating an inoffensive bird-like man and a red-faced fellow in tweeds and a striped tie. 'You've got the professor.'

'Well, my boy,' started the jovial professor amiably, pushing a bottle towards me. 'What do you think of that?'

'Fibroids, sir,' I replied proudly.

He frowned. I was puzzled. My answer, impregnably correct, had not gone over too well.

'And that?' asked the jovial examiner, pushing across another bottle.

'Normal ovary, sir.'

He scowled. The bird-like man laughed. I was mystified.

'How would you treat a case of endometriosis?'

'Progestogens, sir. But if I may say, sir, the results are often disappointing.'

My examiner glared. The bird-like fellow laughed heartily, slapping his thighs, taking off his glasses and wiping them.

'Have I said something wrong, sir?' I asked.

'Not professionally,' my tweedy examiner snapped.

'But I don't think you have much future as a gynaeco-
logist.'

My shamed eyes looked down in confusion. They
encountered a pair of brogues, stout stockings, the hem
of a tweed skirt. It frightened me off gynaecology for the
rest of my career, and off medical women for life.

Richard Gregory

NEUROPSYCHOLOGIST AND AUTHOR

As a junior Fellow of Corpus Christi College, Cambridge, my wife and I invited the newly appointed Master and his wife, Sir Frank and Lady Lee, to dinner at our house. We were the first to invite them: it was a great occasion.

Hours before they arrived, I put two bottles of carefully selected wine in front of the gas fire to warm. When the moment came for dispensing the wine, with due flourish and aplomb I picked up the first bottle, which seemed painfully hot. Moving correctly to Lady Lee's right shoulder, I poured her glass: nothing happened. I had forgotten to take out the cork. Putting the bottle hastily on the table, I pulled the cork and a cloud of steam shot out, immediately followed by a never-ending geyser spout of boiling wine.

The Lees found this extremely funny, and we were good friends ever after – in spite of the episode which occurred the following week.

I visited Lady Lee in the Master's Lodge, which was being decorated, as is the custom with a new mastership. The sitting room was being painted: I think blue in one half, and mud-brown in the other. Pointing to the blue, I said, 'What a super colour ... great that you're getting rid of that brown.' Lady Lee suddenly had a markedly contorted expression, and indicated with a tremor that the brown was her new paint, replacing the faded blue.

Equally accidentally, I managed to drop exactly the same brick to friends who took over Profumo's house in

Regent's Park when they were decorating *their* new sitting room. The only possible reaction is Dropped Brick Bluster.

 If you think we have published two similar examples – it is Richard Gregory obviously to whom Joyce Grenfell was referring – this page will serve as an awful warning to those who speak before they think about friends' decorating talents.

Leonard Belson

OPTICIAN

Many years ago, when completing my year of pre-regis-
tration training, I was working in the Orthoptic Clinic of
the London Refraction Hospital with a fellow graduate.
This particular clinic accepted patients suffering from turns
in one or both eyes and general malfunction of the eye
muscles, who would be considered for treatment by eye
exercises or, perhaps, surgery.

At this clinic, my partner and I were instructed to
measure the degree of turn of each patient, which was
accomplished by the patient having to peer down a tele-
scope-like instrument while we, hopefully, did the rest.
Dressed in our clinical white coats, trying to appear older
than we were, feeling most important and fired by enthusiasm, we called for our first patient. This large dock-
worker, complete with twisted ears and bent nose, burst
through the door as if commencing a fifteen-round heavy-
weight contest with Muhammed Ali – and looked as if
he would win inside the distance. One quick glance at his
eyes, however, revealed the weakness, they were completely crossed and staring at each other.

'Sit down,' said my partner politely. 'We are just going
to measure your eyes.'

'Right'o, guv'nor,' replied our jovial friend.

Whereupon my partner pointed to the instrument
through which our patient was expected to look and said:
'Just squint into this now.'

Stanley Baxter

COMEDY ACTOR

Perhaps the reason that I always found Oliver Hardy funnier than Charlie Chaplin was that that apathetic figure dropping bricks was basically sad, and the humour wistful rather than hilarious. But Ollie had pretensions to gentility. His fastidiousness before a fall was irresistible.

On my first visit to Manchester before the opening of a show there, I saw rolling towards me the stocky figure of a man I knew well. But what was his name? I decided he had been a stage-door keeper somewhere – heavens – was it Newcastle? – anyway I mustn't sweep past. He'd be offended. It's a situation we have all been in, and I claim no originality in coping with it like everyone else does. A burst of warm greetings, and pray the subsequent conversation will bring the name – the place – all flooding back ... We shook hands.

ME: Hell – oh!

HIM: Hello.

ME: How nice to see you again. It's been a while hasn't it? Are you living here?

HIM: Aye.

ME: But you're ... er ... still connected with the business?

HIM: Oh, aye.

ME: I'm opening at the Opera House tomorrow.

HIM: Well, good luck then.

(It was at this point that I realized I was talking to Albert

Tatlock of *Coronation Street* and he must think me insane.)

ME: Thanks, old man, I shall need it. Congratulations on your show, it's my favourite programme.

HIM: Thanks.

I shook hands even more effusively and left.

Lord Carnarvon

LANDOWNER AND RACONTEUR

I was at Royal Ascot in June 1933 and was asked by the late Sir Hugo Cunliffe-Owen to meet three distinguished Chinese gentlemen outside the weighing room after the first race.

Having won £1,000 on this race, I was thoroughly exuberant. I greeted these gentlemen by saying, 'How velly, velly nice to see you – I think you might likee see nice weighing room?'

To my horror, one of the Chinese remarked to his friends, 'How very curious Lord Carnarvon should think that we prefer to be addressed in pidgin English.' At which I blushed furiously and felt that I had made the biggest gaffe and *faux pas* of all time.

George Weidenfeld

PUBLISHER

Asked by my debonair host at a small, urbane dinner party how young British novelists compared with, say, their German or American counterparts, I held forth passionately on the great stylistic merits of young British writers, who had an admirable sense of form, of words and of language, but often lacked experience of life or even curiosity, perhaps due to class-bound and stereotyped upbringing, whereas their German and American coevals, while lacking elegance or tuition, had a vast appetite for life as well as rich experience.

'Take young So-and-So,' I said, 'he can only write about his family, neighbours in the country and his one or two love affairs.' Carried away, I recounted a rather sad plot involving a beautiful girl made unhappy to the point of near insanity by the narrator of the novel in question. I sensed a sudden drop in the convivial temperature, saw glances exchanged between the host and his tense, beautiful, new young wife, and realized – too late – that she was the central figure, the heroine/victim of the novel's plot.

Frederic Raphael

BIOGRAPHER, NOVELIST AND PLAYWRIGHT

They had taken a house next to us on the beach, an American family with what seemed innumerable children: his, you understand, and hers, as well as theirs. It would be unfair to call them noisy; deaf to call them silent. We nodded politely when it was unavoidable, but we avoided them when it was not impolite. As the days passed, however, we became more sociable.

The mother, Dixie, was a woman in her substantial fifties, handsome, and eager to drop the names of notable friends and acquaintances. She seldom listened to what you said, yet she was an eager conversationalist: she liked to talk. In the evenings people would walk along the beach from the café further down towards the village, strangers and habitués. The girls were sometimes pretty, sometimes they were not. One evening I was sitting with Dixie by a sandcastle some of our children had constructed and admiring the girls (when they were admirable) while she told me the problems of her first marriage. The girls were not always wise in the degree to which they exposed themselves to public view. A large female in a small bikini wobbled towards us.

'How would you like to have to look at that every night?' I said.

Dixie was speaking of a meeting she had had or at least attended with Secretary Kissinger, but she now looked up to observe, 'Oh, that's Hannah.' And as Hannah came closer she gave a sudden smile of recognition and called 'Mother!' The girl was sixteen and she had just arrived after staying with some people further down the coast.

As they embraced I produced the lamest cover-up I could think of, and the only one: 'I wasn't talking about *Hannah*,' I said, 'I meant that girl,' and pointed down the beach, where a rather attractive, bespectacled girl was ambling along. I don't think Dixie ever allowed herself to hear that particular brick-drop, clangorous though it was in my own ears. As for Hannah, though she certainly never heard it, she has had her revenge. Today, I am told by my own vigilant children, she is one of the highest-paid models in Manhattan.

 We included this brick, not only because of its happy ending, but also because of the author's unquestionable style!

Lynne Reid Banks

NOVELIST AND PLAYWRIGHT

I've spent my life dropping bricks and could easily fill this book with mine alone. During my seven-odd years with ITN I used to boob so regularly that whenever laughter was heard from the little theatre where rushes were seen, word would go out that Lynne had done it again.

One of my prize bricks occurred during an interview I did with the wife of the then Swedish Ambassador. The story was something about ambassadorial social life and how much entertaining had to be done in embassies. 'And tell me, Mrs Björgensson (or whatever her name was),' I asked, 'does your husband have big balls?'

Another time there was a smallpox scare and everyone was queueing up at health centres to be vaccinated. I stood outside with the crew and interviewed people as they emerged.

One little girl said, 'Have you had your sweetie yet? I got a sweetie after.'

'No,' I replied cosily, 'but then I haven't had my prick yet either.'

Of course they were all harmless enough. The dropped bricks one really hates to remember afterwards are the ones which could have hurt people. In the days when the old Stoll Theatre was still in Holborn, right next to our offices, I once had the task of going to collect Vivien Leigh after her show and bring her along to the studio for a live interview at the end of our late news bulletin. The occasion

was her interruption of parliamentary proceedings on behalf of the St James' Theatre, when she was escorted out of the Strangers' Gallery by Black Rod.

I had to bring her in by a deadline, of course, and she very nearly drove me to distraction by refusing to hurry. Hat, gloves, jewellery, perfume, a drink, etc, etc, all had to receive close, critical attention. Visitors had to be greeted and, finally, when I was practically dancing with impatience and we had about three minutes left, she insisted on going out by the stage – instead of the pass – door in order not to disappoint her waiting fans and to sign some autographs.

In the end I got her up to our eighth-floor studio with about one second to spare. Then I bolted down to watch on the newsroom monitor.

The moment the interview was over I burst out with my tale of exasperation to the crowd round the set: 'My

God, what a woman. She nearly sent me round the bend
…' And turning to address the chap standing behind me,
who I had supposed was a colleague, I found myself face
to face with Sir Laurence Olivier. He had stepped over
from the theatre to see his wife's interview.

Eric Ambler

NOVELIST AND SCREENWRITER

My father, a kind man and one of infinite tact in most circumstances, was a multiple brick-dropper of an unusual sort: he had a habit of asking after the dead.

The trouble was that he had too many friends; not too many for his liking or his good, but too many for a memory unequal to the peculiar demands he made on it. On meeting an old friend after a longish lapse of time, he would always recall instantly that the friend had some relation – mother, father, brother, sister, aunt, uncle, niece, nephew – whose health had been a source of concern. After greeting friend X warmly, he would go on without pause: 'And how, my dear chap, is your uncle doing? Better?'

X would eye him oddly: 'Uncle died last year. You wrote saying how upset you were and sent a wreath.'

'Heavens,' my father would strike his forehead, 'I am sorry. Mind must be going.'

However, the next time he met X the same thing would happen all over again. X was by then usually able to smile at the brick. The third time my father dropped it, it would probably end in both men laughing a little wildly. But not all the victims could smile, much less laugh. Then my father, deeply troubled, would compose elaborate letters of apology; although, as my mother used to point out, there really wasn't much to be said by way of an apology when you could forget a death not just once, but time and time again.

It says much for my father's other qualities that none of the victims, even those who didn't smile, ever remained permanently offended.

Elizabeth Longford

BIOGRAPHER

Thus a lady, being introduced to Margot Asquith, whose son Anthony, a distinguished film director known to the family and throughout the industry as 'Puffin', enquired tenderly after a bird with far less charisma:

'How,' she asked, 'is your little Penguin these days?'

'Staggering around, I imagine,' replied Margot Asquith coldly.

Lord Longford

AUTHOR AND PUBLISHER

Lady Violet Bonham Carter and Lady Megan Lloyd George had been engaged in a violent controversy in the *Daily Telegraph* that morning on the question of which of them had the more honourable father and which father had betrayed the other one.

Arriving at the Guildhall for a banquet that evening, I found myself trying to introduce Lady Violet Bonham Carter to Sir Denis Lowson, now unhappily deceased.

'Denis,' I said, 'I want to introduce to you Lady Megan Lloyd George.'

 An early example of one of His Lordship's bricks — I am sorry we are unable to include a more recent example, while visiting Denmark perhaps? But the Longfords do earn our gratitude as being the most helpful of families.

James Herriot

PRACTISING VET AND AUTHOR

I was pleased when Miss Winston moved into our area. A practising veterinary surgeon is always gratified when a prestigious new client appears to fall from heaven, especially when she is an attractive and charming young woman.

Miss Winston was a dog breeder and her Wire-haired Dachshunds won trophies at Cruft's and all the leading shows. Naturally she wanted the best veterinary attention for her fine and much-loved canine strain and maybe she regarded me with some reservation because, though I love dogs and enjoy treating them, I am primarily a doctor of farm animals. I think she wondered whether I knew enough to deal with her valuable charges.

I set myself out to reassure her, and within a few months had managed to build myself up as an authority, not merely on all dogs, but on the Wire-haired Dachshund in particular. I studied the books and waxed eloquent upon the points of the breed – the evenly tapered head, the straight front legs, the arched neck and level back. I left no doubt in her mind; I was an expert.

The process was all very pleasant, because I found the little animals as appealing as their owner: friendly, good-natured tail-waggers, who submitted happily to my examinations and my hypodermic needle.

Everything was idyllic until I was invited to make the opening speech at a large agricultural show about thirty miles away. I do not need to say that I was invited as Herriot the author and not as the obscure veterinary surgeon I have always been, and after I had said my few words I was invited to the President's tent for refreshments.

The President's hospitality was lavish and I put up only feeble resistance as a long succession of drinks was pressed upon me. After an hour of this I was at my most expansive and, deciding to show my wife round the showground, I floated rather than walked over the grass, taking in the flower displays, the horse and cattle classes, the home produce.

At length we arrived at the marquee which contained the dog show. As we moved along the rows of cubicles, I airily pointed out Dalmatians, Labradors, Poodles and Setters. At the top we turned and my gin-misted gaze alighted upon a group of brown, shaggy little creatures rolling about, biting playfully at each other.

I took my wife by the arm. 'Ah look,' I said, 'What charming Border terriers.'

My words were immediately echoed in tones of the utmost horror.

'*Border Terriers*!!??' and the lady in charge of the dogs swung round to face me.

It was Miss Winston, open-mouthed and aghast, staring into the eyes of her veterinary adviser. Wordlessly I stared back at her, my eyes flitting desperately between her face and the Cruft's Champion Wire-haired Dachshunds gambolling at her feet.

'*Border Terriers*!!??' she repeated incredulously, and I summoned up a sickly smile.

There was a dreadful moment when I almost said something like, 'Well, they're the same colour aren't they?': but, thank heaven, Disraeli's excellent precept, 'Never explain', sprang into my mind and I fled, dragging my wife after me.

But, as I stumbled over the turf outside, one sad thought followed me: I would have to start all over again with Miss Winston.

Tom Stoppard

PLAYWRIGHT

I refuse to tell you about the momentous, humiliating and comprehensively disastrous bricks which I have dropped at regular intervals throughout my life; but here is a modest example of my talent for levelling masonry.

My friend, John Wells, telephoned to announce that he was going to see my play *Travesties* in the company of the man who was to translate the play into French. John suggested that I should show up at the interval in the Manager's office, where an introduction would be effected. Sure enough, at the end of the first act, he appeared in the Manager's office closely followed by a young man who shook me by the hand and announced, 'I loff your text.'

John disappeared to the lavatory and I concentrated my attention on my French translator, who impressed me mostly by his physical appearance – he rather resembled Rudolf Nureyev – and by his dashing French suit. He was apologetic about not being able to understand the play thoroughly at one viewing but said that he looked forward to reading it. I thereupon backed him into the corner and gave him a five-minute run-down on some of the difficulties that he could expect to encounter. I may even have grabbed him by the lapel of his exquisite French suit. He certainly began to look a little wary as I burbled on about the nuances in my lovable text. He began to look a little more bewildered than a French translator ought to look, but I pressed on with an account of the small changes which I intended to make to the play and promised to send them to him at the earliest possible moment.

By the time John rejoined us my French translator was definitely looking hunted, but he didn't seem able to get a word in until John interrupted to say, 'That's not your French translator. That's Rudolf Nureyev.' At this moment there entered another man, in a corduroy jacket, a Gauloise between his lips ...

Alan Ayckbourn

PLAYWRIGHT

I once did make the old mistake of putting the right letters in the wrong envelopes. The first letter intended for two film men who had just wined and dined me endlessly and totally pointlessly, went to my mystified agent; the other letter, intended for her describing the ordeal through which I'd passed, went to the film men.

Ten years later, once more dining with the same two men and on the silence caused by the discovery that we did not have a film and never would have, one of them began to tell the story about the young writer he had once met, who put the wrong letter in the wrong ... At this point our eyes met in mutual recognition. 'Do go on,' I pleaded, but he refused.

Magnus Magnusson

WRITER AND BROADCASTER

The biggest brick I ever dropped was not a brick at all
– it was a *slate*. But a very important slate. We were doing
a television programme at Dover, about the discovery of
evidence that Dover had been the headquarters of the
Roman Fleet (Classis Britannicus) in Britain. The pride
and joy of the excavators was a magnificent red slate
clearly marked with the Roman initials C.B.

As it was handed to me, I dropped it. SMASH! And it
broke right across the precious initials.

I didn't feel much like 'Mastermind' at that moment I
must say.

I never knew Mr Magnusson was supposed to be
the Mastermind, but he has earned our gratitude,
if not the Lalique Goblet.

Clement Freud

MEMBER OF PARLIAMENT, WRITER AND BROADCASTER

I was young – which is some excuse I hope.

At a cocktail party I saw a couple sitting in a corner of the room and I approached them, gave them my second-best smile and asked whether I might get them a glass of wine.

The wife looked at me, raised two fingers of her left hand, touched her husband with her right index finger, brushed her thumb across her wrist, then placed the backs of her hands alternately against her chin and said, 'No thank you.'

So I offered to get them some canapés. Similar gestures followed: two thumbs made a V, index finger was stuffed into fist; middle finger held against nose ... then, 'No thank you very much.'

I sat next to her at the table and asked whether she had ever tried this, and beat out a pat-a-cake drum solo with two fists and an occasional palm, followed by both little fingers plunged into my ears.

'No,' she said, 'actually my husband is deaf and I was explaining your questions to him.'

Reginald Bosanquet

TELEVISION NEWSREADER AND WRITER

I was in an Italian restaurant in Chelsea, when there entered a friend whose name I could not for the life of me remember. I called the Head Waiter and asked him to discover, discreetly, who he was.

'Donta worry, Mr Pussycat, I finda outa for you.'

'Yes, but be tactful. Don't let him know it's me.'

'Donta worry, I be sola discressione.'

Two minutes later I received a note saying: 'Dear Reggie, I *always* remember your name because I see your face on the box and because of the women whose company you keep – David Twigg.'

I did the only thing I could – arose and went to David's table.

'What,' I asked, 'did he say?'

'He said,' replied David, '"Mr Bosanquet say you his besta friend but he forgetta your name."'

Ernest Marples

POLITICIAN

I think the biggest and finest clanger I've come across was one which was dropped on me. A bachelor friend invited us to dine one evening and we accepted the invitation. Forgetting the time at which we were asked, my wife rang up her host, who answered the phone and, apparently believing himself to be speaking to his own aunt, whom he had also invited, he said, 'Dinner's at eight, Auntie, and by the way, I've invited the Marples. Can you bear it or are they absolutely your *bêtes noires*?'

My wife luckily was speechless and replaced the receiver.

Life with Neil

As this book has been compiled to aid the National Society for Autistic Children, it might be helpful to describe briefly what autism is and to give some idea of what life is like for one autistic person and his family.

Autism is a syndrome present from birth or beginning almost invariably in the first thirty months of life. Responses to auditory and visual stimuli are abnormal and there are usually severe difficulties in the understanding of spoken language. Speech is delayed in developing; if it does develop, it is characterized by echolalia, the reversal of pronouns, immature grammatical structure, and inability to use abstract terms. There is generally an impairment in the social use of both verbal and gestural language. Problems in social relationships are most severe before the age of five and include an impairment in the development of eye-to-eye gaze, social attachments, and co-operative play. Ritualistic behaviour is usual and may include abnormal routines, resistance to change, attachment to odd objects, and stereotyped patterns of play. The capacity for abstract or symbolic thought and for imaginative play is diminished. Intelligence ranges from severely subnormal to normal or above. Performance is usually better on tasks involving rote memory or visuospatial skills than on those requiring symbolic or linguistic skills.

Neil is now twenty-two years old – he is handsome and immature, sometimes sad and frustrated, often cheerful and content but always needing understanding and guidance. He is now one of the first residents in a community specially created for autistic people and the following anecdotes, which first appeared in Communication, *the magazine of the National Society for Autistic Children, were collected by Neil's mother over several years of his life.*

Mother, bustling about with a book called *What to Look For in Autumn*, some shrivelled nuts of doubtful species, a pencil and paper: 'Now, Neil, what are we going to do today?'

Neil, after careful thought: 'Well, I'm going to twiddle my shoe-laces.'

*

Neil: 'Mother, look into the mirror over your shoulder and walk into the lounge backwards and see if you can make today into yesterday.'

Mother makes it a rule never to refuse any request which seems reasonable (by autistic standards, of course), so she does this scary task and trips over the rug.

Mother: '***** ***** *****.'

Neil, virtuously: 'It's rude to swear.' *He* should know.

*

Neil: 'Mother, come into the cupboard under the stairs.'

Mother, conforming to the above rule of 'reasonable request', does so rather reluctantly as the cupboard smells of old Wellington boots, and spiders lurk there: 'Just for two minutes then.' Having second thoughts, 'Why, Neil?'

Neil: 'To see if it is more lonely in there with Mother and two transistors and a cassette, or with two transistors, a cassette and a light on.'

*

Neil: 'Mother, what is the smallest thing you can hold between your finger and thumb?'

Mother, after innumerable half-witted guesses: 'I give up.'

Neil, triumphantly: 'A piece of air.' Followed by: 'Why is it we can hold the infinity of small things between our fingers and thumbs but not the infinity of big things?'

Mother cannot answer this and pleads exhaustion. She has, however, bought a book entitled *Philosophy Made Simple*, which is becoming a second bible.

Neil's brow is furrowed with thought, which can be a danger signal: 'Why do five pins seem a little, but five elephants seem like a lot?'

Mother reaches for her book – this must come somewhere between 'Socrates' and 'The Use of Reason' or, on a different level, somewhere near 'How many angels can dance on a pinhead?'

*

One has to be absolutely specific with autistics as a rule – they are, as one eminent French philosopher said, 'primitive logicians' and sometimes they do not bother to carry the thought process just that one stage further.

Father: 'Make a pot of tea, Neil, there's a good lad.'

Neil agrees and goes off to the kitchen. He comes back ten minutes later.

Father: 'I asked you to make some tea, Neil. Where is it?'

Neil, hurt: 'It's in the pot, of course.'

*

On the same theme. Neil had washed his hair in the bath before going to the Church Youth Club. Mother tends to nag him as she hates arriving there late when the other people are on their knees – as often happens because Neil tends to leave things to the very last minute.

Mother: 'Hurry up, Neil. Use my hair dryer to speed things up a bit.'

A few minutes later, her attention is caught by a neighbour calling something and pointing up at the bedroom window, where Neil is standing stark naked elegantly holding up one arm and drying underneath with the hair-dryer.

Neil: 'Well, you didn't say which hair, Mother.'

*

After a late night, Neil stumbles downstairs to greet the day unshaven, hair on end, bare feet, red shirt covered with white paint, jeans with a broken zip, stretching and yawning.

Mother: 'Hurry up and get washed, shaved and changed. We're going out.'

Five minutes later a vision appears in green velvet trousers, Mother's cheesecloth smock, an enormous sparkling star of David round his neck, several rings, the merest trace of – can it be lipstick? – and trailing clouds of glory (in this case Chanel No. 5).

Mother, trying not to laugh or panic: 'That's a bit too smart, Neil. Just your ordinary gear.'

Neil, marvelling at his own virtuosity: 'I seem to go from one extreme to the other.'

*

One day Mother bought a rather revolting pair of pink rubber gloves, so that the dye she uses on her hair would be mainly confined to her head instead of staining her hands and nails the usual rich shade of indigo. A startled squawk from the bathroom tells her that Neil has made a discovery of some sort, and an unwelcome one at that.

Neil, in squeamish tones: 'Mother, whose hands are these?'

*

At a church service for handicapped people Mother and Neil were sitting in front of a severely mentally-handicapped young child who made a distressing high-pitched bleating noise every time there was a lull in the proceedings.

Neil: 'Mother, there's a baa-lamb at the back of the church.'

Mother: 'Hush.'

A good loud hymn followed and then another quiet spell, prayers.

Neil: 'I didn't know sheep came to church.'

Mother: 'Shut up.'

Then there was another hymn, followed by some decidedly louder and firmer prayers.

Neil: 'Perhaps it's the lamb of God.'

*

Neil looks everywhere for the young curate who used to take him to Youth Group but who has moved to Liverpool – however, he has promised to come to the church service.

Neil, distressed: 'My Reverend hasn't come after all.'

Mother: 'Yes he has, but he looks different. I'll explain later. He's at the back.'

Satisfied silence, but not for long. John, who formerly had very long hair and a beard, is now short-haired and clean-shaven. He smiles at Neil.

Neil: 'He *is* different – he's got new teeth.'

*

Mother, firmly: 'Now, Neil, no funny business about "Give us this day our day in bed".'

Neil, virtuously: 'No, no funny business ... "Our Father which are in Heaven, Hallo to Thy name" ...'

This, however, turns out to be a genuine mistake, since Mother had only taught him The Lord's Prayer by repetition, and it was such a joyful 'Hallo' anyway, almost akin to 'Hallelujah', that all is forgiven.

*

At tea after the service, Neil, who is by nature a collector (as, indeed, so many autistic people are), is busily engaged in rounding up as many clerics of all denominations as he can for *his* table (High Table?) rather in the manner of a sheepdog rounding up his flock.

Finally he collapses with a happy sigh: 'Good, we've got them *nearly* all on our table.'

*

Neil goes to Young Christian Fellowship meetings on Sunday evenings. Mother takes him there and some kind person brings him home – eventually. He often tells people that he lives in different places, because he enjoys a run round in a strange car. Bewildered strangers here and there have had him deposited on their doorsteps, so, to save embarrassment and petrol, a rota has now been made up. But, before this came into operation, he slipped out of the Club one evening and was luckily met by a friend of Mother's who asked him where he was going.

Neil: 'To the Eagle and Crown.'

Friend, surprised: 'Why?'

Neil: 'I got a bit bored, so I'm going for a pint of special mild.'

The 'special mild' is indeed very special – a Coca-Cola topped up with lemonade and looks like the real thing, so that on Saturday nights, when Mother takes him to the local pub, he looks like 'one of the boys'. Mother remonstrated with him forcefully when told of this escapade.

Neil, with a world-weary sigh: 'The trouble is, Mother, that you can't trust me, can you?'

*

Neil, for the thousandth time: 'If there *was* a colour darker than black ...'

Mother: 'Neil, for the thousandth time, there *is* no colour darker than black.'

Neil, coaxingly, bulldozing his way through Mother's reluctance to give way on this as she sees all sorts of traps ahead: 'Just *pretend* there is then.'

Mother, exhausted: 'OK, just pretend – but remember there *isn't*.'

Neil, triumphantly: 'Well, if there were a colour darker than black, I would paint the walls, the ceiling, the floor, the windows and the door of the bathroom in it – and *then* I'd paint the bath and washbasin *black* to brighten up the room.'

*

Neil: 'Mother, if it could be later than midnight, how late would it be?'

Mother: 'It can't get later than midnight. After 12 p.m. it is the beginning of the next day.'

Neil: 'Yes, but *if* ...'

*

Neil had for many years a plastic lion with a fur fabric skin and a fluffy mane to make it more cuddly, but he never really liked it. One morning Mother went into his bedroom and found the poor animal completely stripped of all its fur and a repulsive naked orange body in full view.

Mother, sternly: 'What is this?'

Neil, with cheerfully innocent expression: 'It's a peeled lion.'

*

Father, from upstairs: 'I thought I asked you to put me out a clean pair of socks, Neil. All I can find is one blue sock and one red one.'

Neil, delightedly from downstairs: 'I've got a pair just the same, Father.'

*

Many years ago on holiday in Scotland Neil, Mother and some friends from the boarding house where they were all staying went up the glen to paddle in the burn – but they didn't paddle for long. Another form of animal life had beaten them to the chosen beauty spot. A hurried retreat. The kind landlady, possibly dismayed at this sudden return of her guests before the cleaners had had time to finish their operations, asks why they were back so soon.

Neil, with venom: 'We were attacked by an infinity of small animals.'

Landlady: 'Och, the poor wee soul is covered in midge bites.'

*

At the zoo – well, so many things always happen there – just one instance. Neil is gazing at the elephants.

Keeper: 'Do you like them?'

Neil: 'Yes, but they need ironing.'

 Remember them both when you finish this book.